# Karma & Reincarnation *in the* Animal Kingdom

"Where else could you read that ants emanate an energetic plasma in waves that radiate pure sweetness and love, or that an anthill is a single Atman comprising 2,800 ants, or that when an ant reincarnates as a stone it is rose quartz and as a plant it is a rose? Barreto is true to a mix of anthroposophical, theosophical, Hindu, Taoist, and other traditions and lores as he blends them in a journey through the interdimensional goings-on of other animals that humans blithely miss."

RICHARD GROSSINGER, AUTHOR OF *BOTTOMING OUT THE UNIVERSE* AND *DREAMTIMES AND THOUGHTFORMS*

"If Steve Irwin, Thoth, Charles Darwin, and Saint Francis were to have collaborated on a book about the spiritual origin of species, I suspect it would look very much like *Karma and Reincarnation in the Animal Kingdom.* Barreto envelops a refreshing wisdom and enlivened framework of metaphysical languages in the animal kingdom. Through myth, tradition, science, and story—combined with the talent of his edgy brand of psychism—the reader transcends into the spiritual realm of animal Jumanji."

RUSLANA REMENNIKOVA, SOUND HEALER AND ANIMAL WHISPERER

"While one may not adhere to all of Barreto's meticulously and well-expressed ideas, he successfully shakes up our anthropocentric belief, and what could be more welcome?"

CHRISTOPHER FREELAND, AUTHOR OF *OTHER-DIMENSIONAL ENTITIES*

# Karma & Reincarnation *in the* Animal Kingdom

## The Spiritual Origin of Species

**A Sacred Planet Book**

David Barreto

Destiny Books
Rochester, Vermont

Destiny Books
One Park Street
Rochester, Vermont 05767
www.DestinyBooks.com

Destiny Books is a division of Inner Traditions International

**Sacred Planet Books** are curated by Richard Grossinger, Inner Traditions editorial board member and cofounder and former publisher of North Atlantic Books. The Sacred Planet collection, published under the umbrella of the Inner Traditions family of imprints, includes works on the themes of consciousness, cosmology, alternative medicine, dreams, climate, permaculture, alchemy, shamanic studies, oracles, astrology, crystals, hyperobjects, locutions, and subtle bodies.

Cataloging-in-Publication Data for this title is available from the Library of Congress

ISBN 978-1-64411-813-9 (print)
ISBN 978-1-64411-814-6 (ebook)

Printed and bound in the United States by Lake Book Manufacturing, LLC

10  9  8  7  6  5  4  3  2  1

Text design by Priscilla H. Baker and layout by Virginia Scott Bowman
This book was typeset in Garamond Premier Pro and Gill Sans with Minion Pro used as the display typeface.

To send correspondence to the author of this book, mail a first-class letter to the author c/o Inner Traditions • Bear & Company, One Park Street, Rochester, VT 05767, and we will forward the communication, or contact the author directly at **davidbarreto.net**

# Contents

# Foreword

## Robert Sardello, Ph.D.

With great strength of conviction, I am sure you will find this book stands as the most forceful, most complete, most comprehensive articulation ever written of the beauty, wonder, and importance of the worlds of insects and animals as primary balancers between Earth, the cosmos, and the occupants of Earth.

From the first page, a swirl of amazing capacities of David Barreto's mind move between and among physics, biology, ecology, metaphysics, and phenomenological presence, easily and smoothly, with an accompanying love of the creatures of Earth. It convinces the reader to imagine and feel the creaturely world as composed of the best, closest, most significant, and most important friends—all of them, from the cockroach to the elephant and beyond.

The writing is filled with surprise after surprise, at many levels, which completely alter one's thinking about animals, even those who instinctively and intuitively know the ever-widening destruction of the animal worlds must be stopped. The difference herein stems from the genius of Barreto, originating from a foundation within both a scientific and a metaphysical cosmology that includes a much more refined understanding of energies. The book is thus not a political statement nor an activist statement for animals, but is founded first in love, soul-awareness, and spiritual wakefulness to the subtle energies surrounding and permeating every creature. These invisible energetic activities are the active links between creatures, Earth, and humans, and must be kept in proper balance.

The notion that insect and animal "pests" must be annihilated completely misses the necessary energetic equilibrium they bring to Earth and to humans, energies to elevate overly dense vibrations. The book is thus a response to an inner call that vividly reveals itself when the author speaks of the vital balancing processes of Earth provided by the tiniest insects and the largest animals, described in exquisite detail. An "infestation" by multiple creatures serves as an invitation to look and find what is out of balance, thanking our friends for showing us the imbalance, and allowing us to correct it. The creatures then leave.

The book is scientific, while smoothly and accurately flowing into metaphysical matters such as reincarnation and karma. Metaphysically minded people will be delighted and surprised at the specificity Barreto provides. Reincarnation is simultaneously spoken of in terms of energy shifts of balance—described in terms of electrons and positrons, and the Higgs boson particle, convincing the more scientific minded of the same processes—and in metaphysical terms.

The multidimensional power of the writing is then employed in an equally dynamic and profound consideration of the manner in which eating meat significantly contributes to antimatter in the universe. He does not use his impeccable reasoning to argue for veganism, but rather simply indicates what eating meat does to the physical body and the highly important energies between human beings, as well as the energies of Earth, considering all in tandem with metaphysical implications.

An open secret permeates the book, accounting for Barreto's ability to move so easily between the physical and scientific view into the metaphysical-spiritual view: he is not a dualist! In his version of unified imagination, there is the implicit understanding that the world is also the soul and the spiritual world, the physical world and the quantum world.

An important section of the book demonstrates the fluidity between cosmos, Earth, and underworld that occurs with animal worship in ancient religions. The reader feels, quite suddenly, the overarching importance of animals to all of existence, as these correlations of animals with the gods and goddesses still exist with our soul life. Here, in this section of the book, the usual mind can return very easily and take this as mere history, while the deep imagination of the reader is perhaps reluctantly awakened. Again, the overarching truth comes pouring in: we are not separate from the animals. The animals are not separate from the spiritual worlds. The animals within awakened imagination are soul/spirit presences. The writing is arranged in such a way that the human-centric imagination we inhabit, the now-destructive imagination, undergoes a much-needed reformulation.

Once this imaginal enlargement takes hold of the reader, the more mystical aspects of animals feel to us, and rightly so, real, and present— rather than "just another viewpoint." All through history, up until the modern moment, human kinship with animals figured centrally in the creative human imagination, meaning that, in terms of images, waves, frequencies, forms, and patterns, a vast and great interrelating of human, animal, and world upheld existence. Sometimes this imagination took the form of totems, a kind of morphing between human and animal that can be inwardly listened to and appealed to or appeased. The writing details these kinds of imaginal occurrences, which also include the elementals—animal-like subtle beings in the etheric kingdoms—depicting how these elementals, imaginal but true beings, are guides and protectors acting through the Earth elements, something that is well-known in present-day biodynamic farming.

This section of the book forms a valuable aid in awakening the elemental/etheric imagination. When we see moss covering a rock, it is a delightfully beautiful, even calming appearance. The elemental imagination, though, sees that the rock is turning into a plant, and given enough time, it will. And, according to our brilliant author, as this process is faithfully followed out, stones migrate into plants, migrate into trees, migrate into insects, migrate into reptiles and amphibians. The underlying imagination says that behind what looks like separations are living, animal-like processes of continual movement.

Here our author has moved into animals as extraphysical entities of extreme power. For many ages, this power accounted for the felt presences of animals as guardians. Barreto follows this picture as it guided Celtic and many other cultural collective imaginations. Every animal is a facet of the divine. In later cultures, these animals were called *familiars* and became a central aspect of the magical traditions, and their archetypal essences also recur in alchemy.

Animal as anima, as animation, thus become central to the depth psychology of C. G. Jung and to the archetypal psychology of James Hillman. Thanks to this book I now think it better to imagine the efforts of deep psychology as the re-animation, the re-animalizing of life.

And, while this deepening of the essential, formative presence of animals as archetypal creatures occurs, this writing also brings imaginal expansion of the actual presence of animals, to the point that the reader will begin to feel how ignoring animals also ignores our inherent soul imagination, depriving the soul of its most generative dimension. The soulless butchery of sentient beings reveals a destruction of imagination that leads to equal butchery of each other, because the essential vibratory effect of animals has now lowered the planet's vibratory frequency. No other way out exists but through understanding and taking off our blindfold to the world-regenerative power of the animals.

The large and extensive conclusion of this book concentrates on the changing of ages. Earth is on the cusp of a change of ages from the Piscean Age to the Aquarian Age. This should be a most significant change into an era of collective soul awareness, equality, and even possible harmony. None of these essential qualities can come about through human effort alone without first changing the demented and cruel extinction of something like 4.9 billion fish and aquatic animals and 215 million land animals daily, easily the most shocking numbers out of many such numbers sited by David Barreto (Food and Agriculture Organization of the United Nations, 2011 and 2017).

A "program" of regeneration, our author demonstrates, would

be a project doomed to failure. The animating worlds are already fully present all around and within us, and only need the proper triggering—which is both the intent and destiny of this book.

ROBERT SARDELLO, PH.D., is the author of *Love and the Soul: Creating a Future for Earth* and *Silence: The Mystery of Wholeness*. He is the cofounder of the School of Spiritual Psychology and one of the six founding Fellows of the Dallas Institute of Humanities and Culture.

# INTRODUCTION

# An Egalitarian Perspective on Animal Spirituality

Throughout its history, spiritualist literature has hardly questioned the role played by the souls of animals in the spiritual world, apart from some alleged successive reincarnations. On the limited occasions when animal spirituality has been addressed, the subject matter has customarily been reduced to "evolving beings" or rather mediocre approaches to a certain spiritual "energy" that would animate their physical bodies. Although ancient cultures such as the Hindu and the Egyptian advocated that people could be reincarnated as certain animals (Lipner 2012, 263–65), or that various gods have the figure of, for example, an eagle, or even that such animals were sacred, they failed to examine in depth the intrinsic spiritual significance of the species from an egalitarian perspective. Thus, all connotations of animal spirituality have consistently been complementary to human superstition that was intended to benefit humans' spiritual journey. "Cats attract luck" (De Vries 1976, 85–86); "The Elephant God promotes prosperity" (Brown 1991); "Sacrifice a lamb, for it takes away our sins" (Milner 2010); "This animal is my guardian animal" (Wilby 2005). As per those examples, it is clear that the remote and the contemporaneous religions and cults have systematically objectified animals, distancing "the beast" from "the sublime."

Frequently, mystical liturgies involving animals are designed to support and favor human spirituality, for most of what has been shown or researched regarding animals' souls is that they have been promptly subjected to human worship and how the animals in question may assist human interests.

Various books attempt to address the subject of the "animal," but the content is usually reduced to interminable lists of which animal signifies what in dreams or mythologies, with other materials merely stating that animals reincarnate, albeit in a less complex manner when compared to humans. In other words, what is found only covers the mere use of their symbolism to further assist humans and their journey toward spiritual ascension and mystical studies.

It is, however, relatively easy to have access to the literature regarding ascended masters, angels, and extraterrestrials who typically dwell far away or in distant dimensions. But in modern days, spiritualist groups, the New Age movement, and world religions still seldom debate the significance of animals regarding creation and spiritual enlightenment, reserving such studies to humans only, as though animals were far from being correlated or categorized as kindred spirits.

In both religious and spiritualistic literature and doctrine, karma, universal laws, and altruism seem to only have an effect when the interaction occurs between humans, which wrongfully undermines one's sins or violations against the well-being of animals and their right to live and evolve spiritually.

It has always sounded rather intriguing how humans could articulate such a vast range of spiritual rights and responsibilities for themselves, but chimpanzees, who, according to the International Chimpanzee Chromosome 22 Consortium (2004), share about 99 percent of DNA with humans, have next to no mention in religious and even mystical scriptures.

Upon failing to get the answers regarding animal spirituality to the same depth that they are available when the subject is humans, I decided to deeply investigate ancient civilizations, folklores, and esoteric schools to not only find answers to my questions, but to share with the world how immensely important the presence of animals in the spiritual world is, detaching their existence from the advantages they may provide.

Initially, I used my academic expertise to gather information from ancient cultures, anticipating the poor referencing that those books, scriptures, and oral mythologies could offer concerning the spirituality of animals. The more I deepened my research into ancient world religions, the more it was clear that animals have never had a prominent status or exceptional treatment, even though animal iconography was and still is vast.

I have reread numerous esoteric books from my collection to identify any allusion to the creation and participation of animals in spiritual phenomena. The result was disappointing. The mentions were reduced to lists of animals and how humans could use their symbols, be spiritually protected by them, and how such deities were connected to those animals. The urge to include animals and their spiritual evolution in esoteric and spiritual disciplines guided me to dedicate time and energy to building this work.

Having participated in several spiritualist sessions and having witnessed countless mediumistic activities, I drew a parallel between the spirits of humans and their alleged paranormal behaviors and the spirits of animals, verifying any similarity and discrepancy. A lifetime of reading books on Western esotericism and the supernatural also validated my assumptions in categorizing the spirits of most species found on Earth. It is essential to indicate that the scientific data shown in this work was compared to an esoteric orientation, and that esoteric claims were, similarly, tested with scientific data.

I have spent years examining papers from the most renowned laboratories and universities on the planet to support the claims in this work that regard scientific research, numbers, experiments, names, and historical periods. Holding educational certifications from the Australian National University and Harvard University, I instinctively applied an objective and neutral approach to my research for this book. Therefore, the goal of this work is to altruistically investigate and present the souls of animals through the lens of modern-day and ancient spiritualist outlooks, regardless of what animals may represent to humans and their religiosity.

In addition to gathering scientific and historical information from a variety of sources and conducting a careful analysis of several spiritualist and occultist works, including those of spiritual channeling and automatic writing—writing without the medium's conscious involvement—while writing this book I personally received telepathically transmitted knowledge from a place I cannot describe. I did not notice the presence of any spirit in the process, or at least I was not made deliberately aware of any. Overall, my extrasensory perception complements and aligns the discoveries in this book. Naturally, it is difficult to provide a standardized citation for the information that came to me this way. So, when not otherwise cited, the information described was mentally received. In other words, it came to me telepathically through one form or another.

This book also addresses the spiritual repercussions of meat consumption, referring to various spiritualist and metaphysical explanations. Additionally, I was moved to address the impact that the meat industry has on the spiritual evolution of animals, which is often disregarded by those who profit from such misfortune and consume meat. The societies that view meat and animal exploitation as the norm are also addressed, as they study and practice religion and various forms of spirituality, yet choose to ignore the very laws and teachings they claim to obey.

Since astrophysics and cosmology are present in most of my works, I have dedicated the chapters of this book to the scrutiny of those sciences in an attempt to find common ground and theoretical methods to equate animals to humans.

The composition of animal spirits is analyzed in conjunction with how they evolve spiritually and physiologically. I will elucidate what animals do on the astral plane and how karma interferes in their lives. I will also indicate the psychic powers that various species enjoy in the chapters ahead.

This work focuses on all species of animals, without prioritizing one or another species. The metaphysical implications and symbolism in the existence of various animals on this planet are to be interpreted, justifying why absolutely all animals are of unquestionable importance for the Earth's spiritual evolution. Taking advantage of an association between modern physics and metaphysics, I endeavor to indicate how balance in the terrestrial psychosphere can be achieved through the fraternal treatment of animals, referring to divine science as a form of undebatable intelligence in its creations. Finally, this book addresses the awakening of a new astrological era, where animals will have their earthly lives elevated to lasting worthiness and dignity.

# PART I

EXPLORING THE SPIRITUAL
NATURE OF ANIMALS

# The Soul

## THE SOURCE

The creation of a spirit emerges from a creative source, which may be characterized as "God." However, any attempt to explain God is challenging and rather ambitious, as the concept of "God" is inevitably subject to the conditioning of the physical brain. The physical brain, in these terms, exemplifies a reduced valve of consciousness (Koch 2004, 105–16). In other words, the physical brain is the materialized version of consciousness, albeit in a much more reduced constitution, for the experiences in the physical realm.

The physical brain may be considered as a reductionist valve because it reduces perceptions of the environment. When sound is heard, or an image seen, or when smells are recognized, the brain processes and decodes that information exclusively based on the material environment that surrounds it. Thus, the brain is a reader of physical phenomena, and therefore it translates vibrations and matter into observable reality. Each and every explanation about God will depend on the physical brain, which will impeccably try to understand God, albeit in a physical, observational way.

Consciousness is manifested physically as the brain, and although consciousness is able to acquire significantly more information than its material counterpart, it is still in the early stages of spiritual enlightenment. This means that, despite enjoying a broader perspective, human consciousness (spirit incarnate as human) still needs to evolve considerably before being able to fully understand God.

Explaining the concept of God to a physical brain is comparable to explaining electricity to a child, whereas explaining electricity to an electrodynamics scholar is comparable to explaining God to an evolved consciousness. To fully comprehend God, an unimaginable capacity of understanding would be required by the spirits who are incarnated as humans today. However, considering that even spirits with immense evolutionary progress, such as Laozi or the Count of St. Germain, still do not understand God in its total magnitude, nevertheless, they are well on their way to doing so.

Criticism based on Cartesian logic and materialistic sciences alleges that the existence of God cannot be proven (Beyssade 1992, 174–99). However, God should not be evidenced in the material world through the lenses of a microscope, for God is not matter. The use of materialistic theories to prove that a nonphysical being should or should not exist is unproductive and ineffectual.

Intelligence or academic degrees are not prerequisites for the acceptance or denial of possibilities concerning the existence of God, or any extraphysical entity. Correspondingly, microscopes will not see God, satellites will not speak to another dimension, and quantum computers will not contact the spiritual world, as these instruments are *physical* instruments, made in the *physical* world to deal with *physical* phenomena.* The physical brain is composed of approximately 86 billion neurons, yet it is still not able to understand how other planes above the third dimension work, despite having the most complex, technological physical tools at hand.

## CREATION OF THE SPIRIT

The following explanation derives from what a physical brain, as a decoder, may be capable of assimilating. Although creation occurs

---

*Presumably, in the future, enlightened scientists will produce interdimensional or "spiritual" devices, but these technologies are still mere prospects, more specifically associated with the Age of Aquarius.

in the subtle dimensions, this analysis considers spiritual and astral creation, which are the primal reasons for physical matter to emerge.

Source, also called God, is consciousness; therefore consciousness is the creator of reality. Its physical creation occurs at a quantum level; that is, it invariably starts with the fabrication of minuscule particles, waves, and forces before it develops into anything else. These particles and waves will normally give rise to larger and more sophisticated particles and waves (Kardec 1857).

The quantum vacuum is the quantum state with the lowest possible energy. Generally, it contains no physical particles, and according to quantum mechanics, the vacuum state is not truly empty but instead contains fleeting electromagnetic waves and particles that pop into and out of existence.

The concept of holography in physics refers to a type of particle or excitation that is not physically real but instead is a manifestation of information encoded on a lower-dimensional boundary (Wen 2004). This idea is connected to the creation of matter through holographic particles, which are initially nonphysical excitations of underlying quantum fields. These condense and become tangible as a result of interactions with other fields. The Higgs field plays a crucial role in the creation of matter, giving mass to particles such as the Higgs boson and other particles such as electrons, photons, baryons, neutrons, and protons (Baggott 2012).

At the moment of spiritual creation—that is, of the particles and waves that will not become matter of the third dimension—the Atman is created, or detached from the Source (as described by Rigveda Suktam mandala 10 hymn 97; see Wilson 1866 and Grimes 1996). The Atman can be understood as a holographic particle of God, which will remain holographic forever in relation to the concepts of the third dimension.

The Atman, a divine spark, starts its journey toward evolution before it is connected to any physical form. Although it is considered a divine fragment, at this point the Atman is merely an elementary consciousness. Although it will not acquire physical mass, the Atman can be embodied by denser bodies, granting it the ability to experience existence on other planes of reality and thus accumulate complexity and knowledge. In the distant future, it may then reunite with the Source once again.

Typically, this primitive consciousness would first appear as an elemental of a certain kingdom—mineral, aquatic, aerial, fiery. (See Silver 1998 for a deeper discussion of elementals.) An elemental evolves in the astral dimensions as an "invisible" part of the elements, until it may (or may not) finally join a rudimentary being in the third dimension. An elemental is a well-structured form of energy with a minor degree of awareness, which dwells among the astral versions of the earthly elements before eventually merging with or migrating to, or as, an animal in the third dimension. Some elementals, however, may never migrate to the physical plane.

All beings that inhabit the physical universe initiated their existence in a corresponding way, originating in one of those kingdoms of matter, and thereby started their evolution of consciousness in more ethereal realms before migrating to matter. These primitive and collective consciousnesses will live among stones, water, gas molecules, magma, and subsequently, among plants and insect colonies. (Take into consideration that "consciousness" signifies a prototype of the spirit.)

In the physical dimension, evolution results as a consequence of the physical conflicts undergone by these beings over the course of thousands of years. As the semiphysical aura of stones, water, and gases, these beings progressively experience physical pressure, temperature variation, radiation, and environmental collisions, which leads the immature consciousness to the acquisition of further complexity. (For more information, see Kardec 1857; Hodson 1952; and Barreto 2019.) In these elementary kingdoms, these beings experience life in the semiphysical dimension for the first time.

As these beings spend a significant amount of time gathering experiences in the more ethereal planes, their Atmans radiate to the rudimentary physical beings nearby that undergo compulsorily varied and sophisticated experiences, as exemplified by the monera, protista, and fungi kingdoms, as well as the plant kingdom and insect classes. These physical beings participate in life by means of fluid exchange, respiration, and an immersed union with the physical world. Plants normally depend on water, air, minerals, and, typically, sunlight. The monera, protozoa, fungi, and especially the insect kingdoms are where the experiences are designed to introduce these embryonic and collective souls to instincts.

The Atman will sail through different nonphysical beings and radiate (influence) various physical species before eventually experiencing life in the physical plane as the divine spark of an individualized animal. The Atman will always conserve the same essence regardless of the species it radiates or the evolutionary level it finds itself in. The essence found in a stone such as black tourmaline works its electromagnetism on what are thought to be negative energies; that same essence may eventually migrate to a plant that, comparable to black tourmalines, absorbs and mitigates harmful energy from the environment, such as a plant like rue. And the essence of rues may likewise animate insects, like dragonflies, who develop similar extraphysical functions to black tourmalines and rues. The evolutionary level advances and the kingdoms vary, but nevertheless, the essence of the being—the Atman—remains unaffected. Notwithstanding one's essence, different Atmans also comprise a variety of essences, such as knowledge, faith, love, and justice. The stone, the herb, the animal, the human, and the angel permanently maintain their essences, either by being influenced by an Atman or by being a vessel for it. Even in the distant future, when these Atmans merge back into Source, they will still remain unique.

The evolution of the rudimentary consciousnesses of animals when experiencing life in matter can be compared to the evolution of the species examined in modern-day biology. And just as some prehistoric animals evolved into bipeds until they reached *Homo sapiens,* the evolution of consciousness and the Atman on this planet occurs in a corresponding and proportional manner. (See Leadbeater 1902 and Barreto 2019.)

## THE SPIRITUAL BODIES

There are several layers within each of the six subtle bodies of spirits that animate humans. However, the variation in the number of subtle bodies in animals may fluctuate, since there is a colossal range of microscopic, single-celled, and brainless beings, as well as some animals the size of or larger than cars, not to mention the hominids, bearers of amplified intellect. A "body" can be understood as a vehicle for another, more subtle body, whereby the subtler body can experience reality on the denser plane. Along these lines, the physical body is a vehicle for the astral body, just as the astral body is a vehicle for the mental body, and so on.

The bodies that are found in both humans and nonhuman animals are as follows:

**The Physical Body:** This is a body that comprises the individual's material components, such as cells, organs, and tissues. The glands, whose physiological function includes producing hormones, are found in the physical body. However, they also work as capturing antennas and projectors of electromagnetism in the etheric body (Xavier 1945). The glands, therefore, personify the bridges that anchor energies of subtle bodies in the physical body.

In unicellular beings, microscopic insects, and marine sponges, the physical body is generally the only sophisticated body that they possess; therefore, only a migrating plasma system envelops them, which still cannot be characterized as a complex etheric body. The plasma system is a magnetic system, like the etheric system is, for both systems are generated by vortices commonly known as chakras. The difference between the two is that the etheric system intermediates two or more systems, like the etheric body intermediates the physical and astral bodies; the plasma system, however, does not have an intermediating function (Maes 1959). The magnetic currents around the living being in question are tenuous early in life, develop stronger in the middle of the being's life, and consequently migrate when the being is near its last moments in life. The migration to other familiar beings happens naturally by physical and biological proximity.

**The Etheric Body:** This body is the semiphysical energy field that lies between the physical body and the astral body. The etheric body has this name because it is considerably subtle and comparable to ether, but it has nothing to do with this oxygenated compound.

This semiphysical fluid is composed of plasma, loose atoms, photons, gases in small quantities, and electromagnetic currents. There are several layers of etheric bodies, some denser than others. The aura, which is seen via psychic ability, is part of this body. This body can be understood as a "glue" located between the physical and the astral bodies, and is dissolved after physical death (Maes 1964).

The etheric body is the most complex body in beings such as insects, jellyfish, starfish, and many ordinary fish. In these animals, the etheric bodies host information about the species they are affiliated with and inhabit. Their migration occurs purely in the form of waves to other beings at the time of physical death. The migration of the etheric body is a morphogenetic field* process, which for these animals is the only mechanism of "reincarnation" to other animals of similar physical sophistication.

Substantial parts of the chakras are located in the etheric body. However, the majority of these energy vortices continue to exist in disincarnated spirits, although their aspects and functions are different from the chakras of an incarnated consciousness.

Most of the seven main chakras of dogs, cats, and other quadrupeds easily connect to telluric energies, as one of their sides faces downward. When the spirits of dogs and cats no longer reincarnate into quadruped animals, but into biped beings (either on Earth or elsewhere), their main chakras shift horizontally. Their four paws on the ground not only reinforce their relation to earthly life but also serve as valves that exchange etheric energies with the ground. Most animals have their three lower chakras as their vital chakras, which are designed for the nature of survival, such as eating, self-preservation, and reproduction.

---

*The morphogenetic field is a hypothetical field that would explain the simultaneous emergence of events in noncontiguous biological populations. It describes a kind of instinctive "collective consciousness" of the populations, or the idea of mysterious telepathy-type interconnections between organisms, as well as the concept of collective memories within species. This accounts for phantom limbs and, according to biologist Rupert Sheldrake (2011), how dogs know when their owners are coming home, and how people know when someone is staring at them from far away.

Fig. 1.1. Illustration of the dog's seven main chakras, where most point downward, exchanging energies with the ground. Illustration by David Barreto.

Animals who purely rely on instincts cannot be considered domesticated, as having emotions for species other than their own is necessary for domestication to begin and unfold. When emotionally connected to humans, a fourth chakra awakens: the heart chakra, which is associated with affection and emotions (Motoyama [1981] 1988). In other words, because domesticated animals develop profound emotions for humans, their fourth chakra is further activated.

**The Astral Body:** This is the original matrix of the physical body, endowing it with functions and aspects. (For more on the astral body, I suggest Powell 1926.) This body also carries the biological records of past lives, such as physical traumas, passions, and toxic molecules, which may be purged in a subsequent experience in the physical plane. The antimatter purged is one of the main components of the so-called negative energy, i.e., nocive energy. The purge is usually the redeeming of karmic debt.

The astral body is made up of multidimensional holographic particles, which include baryons, leptons, and neutrinos. This body is the one that gives physical form to consciousness when it is disembodied.

This body is formed by an identical replica of the physical body, as a hologram that can only be seen in the astral dimension or above. However, the ability of psychics to see astral bodies is usually effortless.

The individual's psyche may shape the astral body, transforming its appearance, which, reciprocally, affects the physical body to exhibit that image acquired on astral dimension. However, mutations in the astral body that may produce alterations in the physical body are reliant on DNA. As an example, if an astral body has developed wings, these will not materialize in the physical body for obvious reasons. When an individual undertakes plastic surgery or dyes the hair another color, the astral body usually accompanies the transformation (Barreto 2019).

When sleeping, the individual typically has this body detached from other bodies, hence the term *astral travel*. However, in astral travel, the projector's conscious mind is awakened and, accompanied by the astral body, controls it, and thus they "travel" in unison. In ordinary sleep, the astral body is detached, but the mind will not necessarily be aware or remember.

A lucid dream may be perceived as an astral projection. However, this state suggests that the conscious mind has little lucidity, managing to only retain a certain and limited amount of information. Occasionally, the information in the unconscious mind takes shape during ordinary dreams, turning the lucid dream's scarce lucidity into a reverie-like dream. A dream, on the other hand, is often a collection of old and fresh memories that manifest as a scenario during sleep. Most animals have REM-like sleep (rapid eye movement), a sort of sleep phase in which one has vivid dreams. In REM sleep, the eyes move quickly because of thalamic performance, while brain activity is comparable to that of memory (Basheer et al. 2012). Animals that are prone to dreaming are just as likely to experience lucid dreaming, though asking them to recall such an experience is impossible.

The neocortex contains cells that produce sensations such as sights and sounds when no stimuli are coming from outside. To replicate such astral and subconscious sensations, the animal must have a relevant breadth of neocortex to assimilate the signs and sounds coming from another plane and from remote parts of their brains. Since the presence of the neocortex is indispensable for dreams to occur, reptiles, amphibians, and fish do not dream. Keep in mind that, along with the neocortex, animals need an astral body for dreams to occur (Barreto 2019). Allowing that the brain is the physical version of consciousness, albeit in a reduced adaptation, it is understood that animals with an insufficiently developed astral body cannot dream, since the prototypes of their astral bodies do not detach from their physical bodies during sleep and, thus, their instincts still completely dominate the functions of their brains, which do not yet assimilate individuality.

It is also in this body that magic spells against the individual take place. Likewise, this is the subtle body of sensitive mediums that spirits and entities attach to for channeling. The astral body is generally the most sophisticated subtle body that reptiles may own. In species of this class, any auxiliary subtle body, besides the astral, would simply be a set of collective currents and/or embryonic systems of an astral body. Amphibians and types of fish also have this as their most refined subtle body.

**The Lower Mental Body:** This body is a spherical wave that interpenetrates the other six bodies. In most types of mammals, including humans, it is located between the navel and two feet above one's head. This is also an elastic body, which is invariably much longer than the physical body. Although this body is mostly seen as an oval sphere in humans, its form can easily be molded into virtually any form, including that of the astral body.

The lower mental body is responsible for thoughts and reasoning, as the subconscious and the sense of "right and wrong" are the nonmaterial counterpart of the brain in terms of emotions. This body, composed of highly subtle plasma, is where thought-forms are produced, which, once nourished by the astral body, are exteriorized.

This is the most developed subtle body in most mammals and birds at their current evolutionary levels. Domesticated animals, such as dogs, cats, horses, and monkeys, frequently expand these bodies thoroughly during their physical lives.

**The Upper Mental Body:** This body is responsible for the sublime thoughts and ideas detached from materialism. It is also the part of the individual that expresses the essence of consciousness by virtue of one's personality.

The upper mental body is often constructed in a manner that resembles helices or long petals. It is divided into ten parts in humans and three parts in the vast majority of other mammals. These "petals" are connected to other subtle bodies, employing energy cords. Although these petals give form to this body, the upper mental body does not have a defined shape, but appears this way so that humans endowed with clairvoyance can understand it when in a trance or in astral projection (Borsboom 2000).

Helix number 1 is connected to the buddhic body in humans, with a direct tie to past lives of 700 years or more. In animals, this helix still has an embryonic quality. Helix number 2 is linked to intuition, carrying information from experiences that occurred between 300 and 700 years ago. Only a small number of animals, usually quadrupeds, have this helix relatively developed, albeit almost constantly inactive. Helix number 3 is connected to the morals of the conscience, and it contains the memories of incarnations from the past 300 years. This helix attaches to the lower mental body. Mammals—such as dogs, dolphins, pigs, and chimpanzees—have this "petal" comparatively similar to that of human souls. Helices 4 and 7 are attached to the astral body, absorbing and sending information. The process and functionality of these petals in the upper mental body of mammals and birds are identical to their functions in humans. Helices 5 and 6 are connected to the astral body (and prototypes of astral bodies) of all vertebrate animals, in a system identical to the process in humans. Helices 8 and 9 are connected to the Atman body. In animals, these helices are still small sparks in a rudimentary state. Helix number 10 is the center of this fan or flower bud, or the core of this body, where the energies of spiritual healing make their first stop before being distributed to other bodies, including the physical body. Do not confuse *spiritual healing* with *energizing* or *energetic cleansing,* which takes place directly in the astral and etheric bodies. The colors of this body vary from helix to helix in the souls of humans, each color being a sign of the health and state of each body whose specific helix is linked to. In animals, adversely, this "flower" is ordinarily sparkling white with hues of pink and blue.

The upper mental body, which has no material counterpart, is entirely independent of physical existence or the third dimension. It is composed of a high-frequency field that operates in several planes simultaneously. Animals have yet to develop this body and experience most of its qualities; however, it already exists to a superficial degree in most mammals.

**The Buddhic Body:** This body is also known as "buddhi," where memories from the beginning of the individual's creation are stored. This sun-shaped body is an authentic software for recording consciousness. Numerous species of animals have it; however, it is comparable to a wave of information rather than a well-structured body. Thus, the buddhic body of animals may be recognized as a holographic cell that, eventually, will embellish a sophisticated anatomy. All vertebrate animals have this corpuscle in the shape of a small spark, which agglutinates to their other bodies.

The buddhi also functions as a compass that measures when and how a discarnate spirit must reincarnate in order to repair the imbalances in its evolutionary and expanding journey. In animals where such a body is an elementary model, the rhythm in which their astral or etheric bodies should behave is the buddhi's attribution. Moreover, it is through the buddhic body that spirit guides and mentors communicate. The constitution of the buddhi is forged by multidimensional field networks.

**The Atman Body:** In Gnosticism, the "divine spark" is a shapeless entity. It is the first component to separate from the monad, which is a group of Atmans that stem from the "Source" and begin their individual journey. The Atman begins its existence in the divine dimension, then moves into the buddhic, mental, and astral dimensions, where it uses an astral body as its vessel.

All sorts of mammals and birds are Atmans. The Atman is commonly found in animals that have acquired an individualized soul.

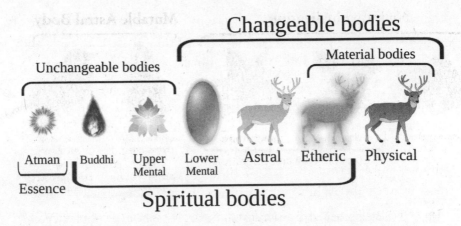

Fig. 1.2. The divine essence, the spiritual bodies, and the material bodies of a large mammal. Illustration by David Barreto.

Unicellular beings and insects, however, are still part of a collective spirit. Although there is no Atman present in such "group spirits," their collective energy and experiences regularly migrate to individualized animals who have just begun their journey as a single spirit. Prior to manifesting in the physical plane in an individualized animal, the Atman radiates to the collective souls of various species, including insects. When the group of insects is ready to move to another realm, their etheric energies are assimilated by the more complex and individualized animals in the physical realm. That is, these insects, as a group soul, "reincarnate" in such a way that their ethers migrate to form the etheric bodies of individualized animals. This migration of etheric energies conserves the experiences and complexities garnered by the insects from previous experiences in matter.

The evolution of animals' spirits in the third dimension occurs proportionally to the "evolution of the species," whereby a given species undergoes adaptive mutations, sophisticating their bodies and senses. It must be stressed that the same process has happened and will continue to happen to humans. Nevertheless, physical changes over the millennia do not happen unexpectedly, but by the influence of the spirit that animates the physical body.

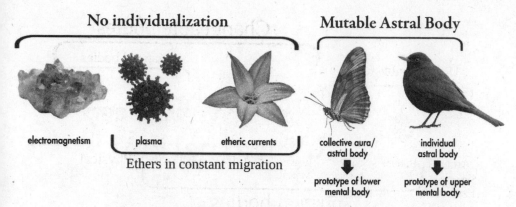

**No individualization**       **Mutable Astral Body**

electromagnetism    plasma    etheric currents    collective aura/ astral body    individual astral body

Ethers in constant migration

prototype of lower mental body    prototype of upper mental body

Fig. 1.3. Classification of the simplest to the most complex types of spiritual energies expressed in the mineral, plant, and animal kingdoms. Illustration by David Barreto.

Sequentially, the evolution of the spirit rises with the knowledge acquired, along with noble principles, such as compassion, benevolence, and empathy. In other words, love.

As an example, the spirits that animate bears, whose Atman origins are identical to those of humanoid spirits, must also develop their physical bodies to obtain enough spiritual expansion, thereby being able to make compassionate decisions and progress to transcendence. It must be taken into consideration that although humans can develop such qualities, a substantial proportion of the world's population remains dormant to them; therefore, being human does not automatically classify them as superior to spirits of nonhuman animals.

The souls of animals, therefore, are notably similar to the souls that animate humans. Many of the spirits that animate humans also initiated their individualized journeys elsewhere in the cosmos, as on other planets, but not necessarily on the physical plane; however, the divine spark of each one was generated in a similar course to that of all existing animals.

# 2 Karma and Reincarnation

Karma, and reincarnation of spirits that animate humans, primarily refers to the repairing of personality imbalances and actions that are necessary for that spirit to learn. The karmic process results in potentially painful experiences, but it also comprises the path to love, charity, knowledge, and the divine law.

*Karma* is a word from Sanskrit that means "action." This is an action that has to be performed or experienced, so one heals their spiritual malaise—that is, the imbalance between the principles of action and reaction, caused by moral failure or misconduct, either in past lives or in their current ones. Karma leads the individual to experience an emotional reaction that is similar to the emotion caused by their action. One does not necessarily experience the very same reaction to the action initially taken, but an experience that emotionally corresponds to the pain one might have caused. Karma can also be reparative, signifying that the individual acts directly in the reaction to "solve" that adverse action previously caused. As a study case: a false priest, a false medium, or an individual with the ability to persuade by the agency of faith may inexcusably direct a devout community to infelicitous paths for their own individual benefit and the gaining of power. This false spiritual leader's karma could presumably be an obligated and strenuous devotion to directing that community to compassionate and loving paths, thus causing a reparative effect on what was originally done. That said, most of the educators and priests who come to devote their lives to teaching humanitarian conduct certainly enjoy what they do, despite its difficulties. Thus, as I explain in my 2019 book *The Supernatural Science,* karma is not necessarily a burden, but a condition (see pages 61–67 of that book). The karma a person goes through is nothing more than rebalancing their vibrational debt in the universe.

As this is hardly achieved due to pungent egos, there is moderate friction as a course of reacting to the impact caused, generating some of what is recognized as "suffering."

Typically, karma is the reaction of an "evil" caused to someone or something, such as the malicious pollution of a river or the cutting of forests for selfish gain. The difference between doing "good" and doing "evil" is that, when doing good, an expansive movement of the spirit is generated, while "bad" actions retain the spirit. Furthermore, the difference between "good" and "bad" is when an individual with the ability to distinguish the two consciously chooses one side. The "good" aims at the benefit of everyone, detached from selfishness. The bad, in turn, is characterized by selfishness, where the benefit is only personal, whatever the repercussions for others.

By doing what is appropriately called "evil," there is stagnation and loss of momentum (speed) in the spirit's evolution, which culminates in involuntary actions caused by one's own conscience that forces the necessary expansion through pain, either emotional or physical.

The more altruistic a person is, the more expanded their consciousness. It expands as a result of benevolent conduct and the knowledge one acquires. This increase in width occurs due to the need of consciousness for greater amplitude for comporting more information (Barreto 2019, 69–72).

The expansion may also be achieved via what can be compared to quantum leaps, when karma is attenuated by appreciable effort or a worthwhile expansion of consciousness in one single life experience. As an example, a heroic act may lead to a quantum leap.*

---

*In quantum theory, the idea of quantum jumps was first introduced by Danish physicist Niels Bohr. The event unfolds when an electron is located in a certain orbit and then it gains a considerable amount of energy, thus jumping to an orbit above. An interesting phenomenon regarding that leap is that when the electron passes from one orbit to another, it simply disappears from the former and reappears in the next, which indicates a leap (Heibron 1985; French and Kennedy 1985, 33–49).

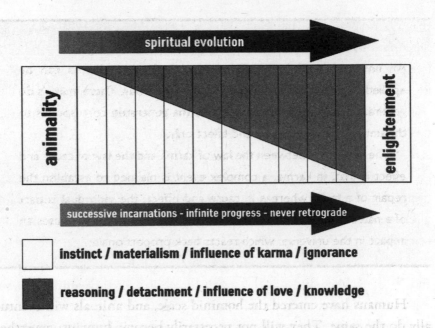

Fig. 2.1. Concept of spiritual evolution on planet Earth.
Illustration by David Barreto.

The occurrence of quantum leaps is, however, extremely rare.

The relationship between human and animal karma is, however, typically generated by various factors. The karmas that most humans collect in their experiences are karmas that redirect and lead these spirits to repair the deviations in the conduct of past or current incarnations. In the case of animals, karma refers to natural actions that lead them to expand their consciousnesses (spirits) because of carnal experiences and, often, through physical pain that also affects humans, but in separate ways. Along these lines, animal karma is just a new experience, instead of a corrective reaction.

Through physical ordeals, the animal learns about all existing feelings, including pain, fear, and anguish. The karmic reasons referring to the pain that animals experience in their journey do not justify, from a spiritual perspective, humans inflicting any harm on them. All animals are incarnated spirits developing the intelligent principle; thus, they follow the same path that humans have been following for thousands of years.

> ## Karma vs. Cause and Effect
>
> An uncomplicated form of understanding animal karma can be applied to all animals endowed with an astral body. These animals do generate karma; nevertheless, the karma generated corresponds to the universal laws of cause and effect only.
>
> The difference between the law of karma and the law of cause and effect is that, in karma, a complex event is planned to establish the repair of a fault, whereas in cause and effect, the individual is part of a natural movement of forces, where what they project causes an impact in the universe, which reacts back proportionally.

Humans have entered the hominid scale, and animals will eventually do the same. They will not necessarily become humans; nevertheless, animals of all sorts will evolve to incarnate in an advanced hominid family, either on this planet or another—though not necessarily on the physical plane.

Although highly intelligent primates, numerous humans use their intellectual capacities to satisfy their egos in barbaric ways. Thus, the karmic responsibility they assume when interfering violently and abusively in the lives of animals is inescapably enormous. On causing suffering via cruelty and exploitation, humans bear the burden of moral deviations and the lack of love that, if not acquired through kindness, must be acquired through the forced purge of these nefarious activities. This purge is also known as "suffering." In other words, the human will unquestionably experience karma for the manner in which they mistreat animals.

Animals feel pain because all beings with instincts experience bodily suffering. That is, lessons for spiritual progress that include physical discomfort are reserved for individuals who still retain their instincts. Before developing instincts, physical pain is not required, just as it is no longer required after being emancipated from them and thus achieving enlightenment by reason and compassion. The physical pains that animals may encounter, such as the natural adversities in the wilderness or diseases, contribute to the expansion of their consciousness, but they do not depend on human actions to occur and therefore will still occur regardless of human activity. That is, humans will not help animals evolve by causing them physical pain, but they will, contrarily, increase their own karma and prevent animals from experiencing every year that their physiology determines (a pig, for instance, can live to be twenty years old, but is taken to be slaughtered before the age of six months in the meat industry).

All forms of malicious suffering inflicted upon an animal, as well as toward another human being, result in serious consequences, including the impediment of the universe's conscious expansion.

The universe expands both spiritually and physically, in what cosmologists call metric expansion. Spirits, likewise the species they animate, evolve on Earth coincidentally.

Animals often experience pains and agonies, and these feelings may lead to a certain expansion of consciousness. Animal karma, therefore, is attributed to the experiences they collect to permanently understand the variation of density between planes of reality.

It is also valid to reiterate that humans likewise experienced extreme pains when their spirits were located in different kingdoms, either on this planet or on another. Physical pain is part of the learning process on the physical plane for spirits who are learning their instincts and thus getting liberated from them. Before acquiring instincts, as in the case of plants, or after spiritual sublimation, as is the case of spirits free from repeated reincarnations, instinct is not present, and hence physical pain or suffering will no longer occur. As the spirit is eternal, the painful period one spends in the third dimension is usually considered short and fruitful.

Nevertheless, the suffering that humans may cause to animals neither helps nor accelerates their spiritual evolution. This is because pain is not invariably mandatory in the animals' current evolutionary course. However, animals *do* need to experience their instincts and nature. Moreover, many of them must experience affection. If animals are denied such resources, their experiences will be incomplete, and more metaphysical debt will be associated with the cruel human being.

Such pains are exceedingly incompatible with the category of experiences they need for their evolutionary progress during a single lifetime. No existent universal or divine laws dictate such suffering as animals endure at the hands of humans. All wickedness against animals is unequivocally the result of sheer selfishness.

## REINCARNATION PROCESS

Spirits can only incarnate in a body that is physically able to perform the functions that consciousness needs to fully experience life. This allows the spirit to absorb and express all the functions it has already learned.

By comparing the body and consciousness of a dog with the body and consciousness of a human being, it is understood that the bodies of each are the physical manifestations of their own consciousnesses. In other words, each spirit will only be compatible with the physical body whose consciousness can exercise all the functions it has already acquired.

A dog's consciousness cannot inhabit a human body before it undergoes a systematic preparation, since the human's consciousness is what generates the human body type. The consciousness that inhabits a human body cannot inhabit a dog's body, as the animal's body does not have the necessary properties to hold or express the consciousness of the humanoid spirit. The reason is that the structural composition of the human body, namely glands, organs, brain functions and the existence of a thick layer of the neocortex, is physiologically more complex than that of the dog.

Although inter-incarnation between the aforementioned species is less common than reincarnation between spirits in the same species group, such a process is possible, given the spiritual arrangements and preparatory measures. Cases of domestic animals passing into the hominid kingdom are usually observed by mediums and explained through channeled messages. Especially after the animal accumulates extensive experience among groups of spiritual rescues, they promote the migration of the animal to the hominid kingdom. It is also common that, in spiritual communities in the astral realms, specific sections are responsible for preparing domesticated animals for future life as humans. However, it is not possible for the human to reincarnate as an animal on this planet.

Human ancestors, such as the *Australopithecines,* the *Homo erectus,* and the *Homo sapiens,* have all inhabited physical bodies that matched their respective levels of consciousness. Just as those species evolved into the modern *Homo sapiens sapiens,* so simultaneously did their consciousnesses (Xavier and Emmanuel 1939b, 27–34). Consciousness normally reinhabits the physical bodies of the same species it had in its previous incarnation, which is compatible with their current spiritual evolutionary levels. This is the norm, but animal spirits can also migrate to more complex earthly species closely related to what they might have been in their previous existence. For example, the spirits of wild boars often reincarnate as domestic pigs. Evolution via reincarnation is a gradual and natural process, like the "evolution of species" in biology, albeit nonperpetual.

As far back as 1857, Kardec put forward the idea that spirits of extinct species commonly reincarnate into species that are biologically close to but more advanced than the extinct species. If this is so, evolution frequently parallels itself in both biological and spiritual terms. This was the case with mammoths to elephants, as well as with extinct tiger species to other species close to felines but with more intellect. Extinction of natural origin is essential for the development of these spirits, which mature in more advanced sensory capacities, requiring a more adequate physical body to support such an increase in consciousness. The same principle applies to animals that are victims of man-made extinction. However, the karmic penalties undoubtedly fall on whomever bears responsibility for such abnormal causality.

During the latest period of the Paleolithic Age (2.5m–10,000 BCE), humans considered wolves to be their rivals, as the animals would not only hunt the same prey as humans, but would also attempt to hunt humans themselves. Naturally, wolves would hunt in packs. Nonetheless, some of them eventually started to get closer to the humans, realizing that when they showed a more docile attitude, they could potentially be given leftovers. Because of the approximation between the two species, protodogs first appeared around 33,000 years ago. Those protodogs were smaller than wolves and exhibited a gentler temperament with traits of dependency. Their final domestication occurred circa 14,000 BCE.

During Victorian England, neoteny, which results from the selection of breeds for tameness traits, became common. New breeds of dogs were bred for different purposes, such as hunting, racing, herding, and companionship. The phenomenon of artificially creating new breeds, as well as the natural occurrence of physiological evolution, coextensively accompanied the spiritual evolution of those canine spirits, from wolves to dogs and from the common dog to its subspecies.

The creation of new breeds was not actually an achievement of man but an achievement of the numerous spirits who came to be incarnated in such appropriate bodies. It is worth emphasizing that the artificial creation of new breeds was an effect and not a cause. Humans, in such a context, served to facilitate the arrival of a new era for the canine species. The domestication, tameness, and personality traits that dogs achieved through millennia via either method are solely a reflection of the spiritual journey that those spirits needed to experience. The physically sophisticated brains and the weakening of some of their instincts, when compared to wild wolves, served to properly facilitate the expression of a less animalistic aspect of those spirits, allowing them to fully express their spiritual virtuousness alongside humans and finally progress to higher realms of spiritual evolution.

Reincarnation materializes in different directions, depending on the species. In a species that may only possess magnetic currents involving their bodies as opposed to souls, as is the case with unicellular beings and microscopic insects, reincarnation may initiate even before their actual physical deaths. Although they do not have a complex energetic structure, the plasma surrounding these beings' atoms is collectively magnetized. This means that what has been lived and experienced by those microscopic beings is not lost as an experience, nor is it stored as a memory. The plasma that surrounds collective souls is part of the environment that prepares them to eventually obtain spiritual individuality. Preceding death, the plasma that surrounds a colony migrates to other groups of living beings who are part of collective souls. This migration develops through electromagnetic waves.

Even among animals who are holders of a sophisticated group of etheric bodies or an astral body, which is the case with insects, reptiles, and amphibians, reincarnation also occurs immediately after death. Their reincarnation process is randomized, as their subtle bodies (collectively or not) migrate to fertilized eggs in the first stages of development.

The subtle body of insects penetrates the eggs instantly at the moment of fertilization; however, as part of collective souls, it is not a complete astral body that migrates, but waves of information in the form of vibrating strings. In comparison, collective spirits of snakes only completely migrate to new bodies in the eggs when most of the new animals' instinctual functions are mature. However, at the time of fertilization of the egg, the snakes' astral body, depending on the species, may decrease in size so that it can bind to the embryo's replicating cells.

Moments after physical death, the snake's essence will induce prefertilized eggs with its traits for a new reincarnation process. The time variation that insects, reptiles, and amphibians take to connect to an egg for their group reincarnation ranges from seconds to 170 hours. The more sophisticated the animal's subtle body is, the later they "merge" with another physical body.

These animals' astral and etheric bodies adapt according to the size, shape, and gestational stage of the new physical body, which will be animated in a new life. The process of adapting to the new body is also immediate, and the cords that connect a recently disembodied spirit to a physical body, typically in eggs, are initiated by fine energy threads that connect to each other, like a type of transference system of holographic data.

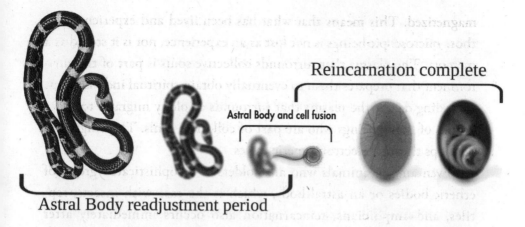

Reincarnation complete

Astral Body and cell fusion

Astral Body readjustment period

Fig. 2.2. Reincarnation process of a snake. The spiritual transfer of snakes (both individually and collectively) to eggs is usually immediate after physical death, where their astral bodies shrink to the size of cells. Illustration by David Barreto.

Following the disembodiment of mammals, their spirits remain in the astral dimension indefinitely. However, in most cases the process of reincarnation promptly begins hours after death for some and even years later for others, as it does for the domesticated mammals.

The reincarnation process, which varies from species to species of mammals, occurs in a similar fashion to the process that humanoid spirits undergo.* The subtle bodies of the reincarnating spirit gradually connect to the developing zygote. The connection between the reincarnating spirit and the embryo is made by fine energetic threads, which influence the dividing cells and, consequently, give the animal its unique features. In this phase, the activation of inherent spiritual qualities occurs, as well

---

*In the case of humans, the process is identical. However, the preparation of the parents' reproductive cells is done even before the spiritual connection to the egg and sperm. As humans reincarnate, among other reasons, to collect their karma and revise family commitments, the spirits of the parents and the reincarnate must initially agree for the pregnancy to occur, where all family members commit to progress and amend previous lives' issues. Only then is a specific sperm activated, as is the egg that it will find. During the process of connecting the spirit to its new physical body in the form of a zygote, thin threads of semiphysical energy connect both the spirit and the dividing cells. This draws the small spirit to intrauterine life, where it falls into a sort of sleep state.

as the activation and inactivation of genes. Until the first moments of gestation, many viviparous animals can still be seen outside the womb of the mother, maintaining the shape of their past lives. Over the course of hours, depending on the species, the animal is immersed in a torpor, where its conscience will remain asleep until birth. The threads that connected the spirit to the embryo, which were previously thin, become thicker and cause an attraction between the two, which culminates in the joining of the spirit to the fetus in its entirety.

Intelligent, emotional, and domesticated animals do not choose to be reincarnated, nor when they will do so. Supported by friendly spirits, their astral meridians are interwoven with the atoms that are going to develop into the glands of an embryo, which gradually start to animate those bodies on the physical plane. As their astral bodies temporarily lose the memories from their previous experience in matter, the new body commences receiving the subtle and unique qualities of the spirit.

The reincarnation context of mammals who have thick layers of gray brain matter, or those with any congenital ability to have an intellect, or be moderately inclined to affection, is considerably refined. Such animals, including chimpanzees, dogs, horses, and elephants, experience a preparatory process before reincarnating. As their astral bodies carry abundant emotional and intellectual experiences acquired in their previous lives, the time they spend in the astral dimension is generally longer than for most other less evolved animals, whose reincarnation is immediate after death.

According to Marcel Benedeti (2012), usually, dogs and cats remain at their owners' homes as if nothing has changed for a brief period after their deaths and preceding a new incarnation (on average, for approximately five weeks). The period in which the spirits of animals remain at their owners' home is orchestrated by friendly spirits. Due to being accustomed to interacting with humans when they were alive, all domesticated animals remain in the homes of their humans for some time after death, and others are taken to spiritual colonies where, in addition to animals of the same species and similar breeds, they can also find the spirits of humans.

After the physical death, it is also common for spiritual mentors to create holographic places and objects familiar to the pet, to make them feel comfortable in the new reality. These holograms are exclusively experienced by the animals' minds.

Occasionally, friendly spirits committed to animals take them to another plane, to experience the place where other animals of the same species are, and where they will stay until the next reincarnation. From time to time these spirits transport them back to the owner's home. Thus, the animals can get used to the new reality without the trauma of separation.

On the other hand, when wild dogs and wild cats die, they are usually reincarnated swiftly after their death, as the noninteraction with humans prompts them to a new experience without depending on interaction with a different species.

In hospitals in the astral dimensions, the disoriented spirits of humans may be aided by the spirits of past pets, who are brought by candid nurses to help the deceased humans accept their condition and reduce their sadness about having died. (It is appropriate to add that spirits dedicated to the cause of animals in the astral dimensions commonly influence incarnated humans, so that they help animals in the physical plane as rescuers and, less frequently, as activists.)

In nature, every species progresses close to other members of the same species. However, when interaction with humans exists, domesticated animals develop affection for another species different from their own. Therefore, these animals greatly amplify their heart chakras, which remain compact in most wild animals as they heavily rely on instincts as opposed to emotional bonds—the main motivator for the expansion of the chest chakra.

It is doubtlessly possible that the human may find the deceased animal in the astral realm, either via astral travel or after their own deaths. It is also natural for the human to acquire a new pet, which could be the reincarnation of an animal they have had in the past. Another common situation involves jointly reincarnating for new experiences together, and although this reunion's potential occurrence depends on how important it would be for the two beings' evolution, this is a common circumstance.

Interestingly, the intrinsic intelligence of animals such as dolphins, crows, and octopuses does not automatically qualify them for a particularly sophisticated reincarnation process, such as the processes experienced by gorillas and cats. Despite being smart and able to reason, they still need to further develop affection. It is, therefore, affection that determines which experience the animal must undergo in the next incarnated experience. The less inclined to affection the animal is, the more random the reincarnation may be. However, the more inclined to affection, the more specific the new experience in the flesh must be, to accommodate the emotional needs of that spirit.

Additionally, even though most animals reincarnate rapidly after death, not all will do so. Some animals, on rare occasions, may take hundreds of years.

Some animals work together with groups of rescue spirits, whereas other spirits of animals join those beings who have never lived incarnated lives. They dwell in dimensions exceptionally close to the third dimension and are customarily called *elementals* of nature. The elementals are responsible for maintaining the balance between the elements of the planet, stabilizing the frequencies between the physical and semiphysical world, and supporting the movement of life. This is partially executed by those animals that are endowed with plasma instead of a sophisticated soul, which are mostly insects, but also some types of fish, amphibians, and reptiles.

The decision not to reincarnate is not an animal's; it is, however, due to a natural magnetic need that their souls or subtle bodies must experience. Occasionally that serves the animal when they are approaching the migration to another realm.

To conclude, wild animals will incarnate into other animals raised by humans, such as cattle; hence, they are no longer being killed by other wild animals, but instead (regrettably) by humans. Upon progressing to another species, the cattle will incarnate into other animals kept in captivity, including domesticated animals. Subsequently, they will incarnate into pets such as dogs, cats, and horses. Finally, at least on planet Earth, they may incarnate as humans after life experiences elsewhere.

Not all animals on planet Earth will evolve through stages in human physical bodies. Many, notably most species of fish and birds, will continue to evolve in paths parallel to the human kingdom.

After completing a relevant level of lessons on the material plane, these animals continue their journeys on the astral planes, reincarnating in the different densities. Some continue their evolution as evolved elementals; others remain as nature spirits until a next evolutionary stage before they reach the *deva* realm (advanced spirits that govern fauna and flora in different dimensions).

The parallel evolution of these species has the same destination of what humans aspire to—knowledge, altruism, universal love, and a return to the Source.

The better humans treat animals, the faster the latter evolve spiritually and progress to another kingdom, such as that of humans, since animals must understand and deeply interact with the human species before they can incarnate as part of them. If animals are mistreated or abused, they will most certainly need more incarnations, until they fully develop emotional bonds. If humans do support animals in evolving, they acquire merits. Nevertheless, if humans delay the evolution of animals by being cruel toward them, abusing them or killing them, they will inevitably accrue karmic debt.

Daily, a small percentage of human births are births of former animals—spirits who were animals in their previous life. Considering that, in the first decades of the twenty-first century, approximately 380,000 humans were born every day, perhaps around 1,000 animals enter into the humanoid kingdom on a daily basis. Not just animals from Earth, but also those from other planes of reality or those who were animals on Earth, reincarnated as primitive humans elsewhere, and then returned to Earth. Human first-timers frequently live shorter lives, or may, occasionally, display physiological anomalies. Most human first-timers were evolved animals or sub-evolved humans on another planet.

# 3  Animals and Metaphysics

Animal metaphysical energy refers to a complex system of waves and quasi-particles that are generated and usually modified by animals' energy fields (the subtle bodies and electromagnetic fields of animals).

## EXTRASENSORY CAPABILITIES

Most vertebrate animals are born with a pineal gland. This physical gland receives the signals of light and darkness from the eyes, thus producing melatonin, which is a hormone related to the sleep pattern. The astral version of this gland, on the other hand, is sensitive to the photons in the electromagnetic field generated and perceived by the physical gland itself. As a result, it produces a wave motion that interferes with the animal's entire electromagnetic field.

The wave interference is established according to the mineral arrangement that composes the apatite in their pineal glands: calcium phosphate, magnesium phosphate, ammonium phosphate, and especially, calcite. The waves emanating from the apatite, thus, vibrate in alignment with the geometric distribution of its atoms. What makes the calcite exceptional is the crystal's ability to generate an electric current. This ability is known as the *piezoelectric effect,* that is, "the ability of certain materials to generate an electric field in response to applied mechanical stress" (Yang 2022).

Due to the pressure that calcium carbonate blades cause on one another, a low-intensity electrical voltage occurs continuously in calcites. When the plates push against each other, they direct the loaded parts to their opposite sides. Thus, the positive charge tries to pull electrons from the inner part of the mineral sheets, while the negative part tries to repel the electrons. In such an alternating transit, electricity is generated. The movement, therefore, replicates a geometrically perfect electromagnetic field, propagating the mineral's atomic arrangements (Guerin, Tofail, and Thompson 2018). In such a way, it can be proposed that the piezoelectric effect* turns the pineal gland into a living being that pulsates the calcite's extraphysical holograms unceasingly. The patterns pertinent to the other minerals present in the crystal also contribute to the symmetrical designs that the gland radiates as an electromagnetic field. The crystals' vibration carries the subatomic information as their "genes," which are all pure, perfectly balanced, and symmetrically aligned.

Although the physical pineal gland interacts with physical electromagnetism via autogenerated electricity, its extraphysical counterpart does so with waves of ether, which are a subtle version of electromagnetism—denser than light but thinner than hydrogen. These ethers, also known as *prana* or *chi,* are distributed via vibrational networks that interpenetrate different planes, including the material third dimension, which is evidently inhabited by physical beings. Even though the pineal gland's piezoelectricity and its electromagnetism seem to conduit considerable nonphysical data, it is the energetic vortex known as the crown chakra where most nonphysical perception is decoded. The etheric dimension is the dimension of energies, aura, holographic particles, and vital fluid. This is the closest subtle dimension for

---

*Although humans also have a pineal gland, an apprehensive intellect or an exalted ego may repress this gland from exercising its fundamental role as an extraphysical antenna. In most humans, metaphysical signals are unnoticed or ignored. Also, when not utterly discredited, intuition is often implied as a mere guess based on memories or physical instincts. Cats may not possess greater psychic abilities than humans; however, they instinctively use their abilities fully, whereas humans use a mental filter before astral information is allowed to blossom.

the inhabitants of the Earth's third dimension. The subtlety of etheric waves can be observed by ordinary humans. That is, an individual does not necessarily need to be a psychic or a medium. Meditation is a resource that can be used so that the "ordinary" individual can become capable of capturing and decoding the energies of other dimensions.

## ANIMAL-ENVIRONMENTAL METAPHYSICAL INTERACTIONS

The ether absorbed and exhaled by insects, as well as by other large animals, will unquestionably interact with humans' electromagnetic fields. Energy travels to the body's organs, tissues, and physical fluids via the energy force centers and the meridians of the humans' semiphysical bodies. This energy, commonly called by diverse cultures *vital energy*, *qi* (pronounced "chee"), or *prana*, is absorbed from five diverse sources:

**The macrocosmic energy:** This energy is the elastic energy stored by an individual's auric field and manifested by the environment in which they live. The interactions with the environment—that is, cleaning the house, self-hygiene, sleeping hours, exposure to sunlight, and material comfort in the home—all affect this type of energy. When the macrocosmic energy of the environment is attracted to the individual's auric field, it immediately becomes part of it. Homes, and without exception all physical vicinities, constitute an electromagnetic network. While the house may be measured as matter and particle, it can also be measured as energy and wave. Thus, these wave fields carry information about the nature of the house's matter and particles. The waves of a disorganized or disheveled house carry information of chaos and imbalance. When chaotic energies are present, the elastic energy of the individual's auric field breaks apart and expands to compensate for the corrosive circumstance, therefore becoming scattered. As all semiphysical elements have limits on how far they can withstand distortion, they are not capable of coping without altering their intrinsic structure. Nevertheless, the essence of elasticity is reversibility; the individual may recover the field's lost particles by simply de-cluttering, replacing an old mattress, or by including plants and pleasant pictures in the house (For more information about macrocosmic energy, see Barreto 2019, 75–76). Such energy is the same for both animals living in the wild and for domestic animals.

**The ancestral energy:** This is the radiant energy carried by light and thermal energy. Individuals inherit it from ancestors by the route of DNA, in electrical signals between the chromosomes' base pairs.

As explained by Kanev et al. (2013), "In complicated molecules like chromosomes, low-lying excited states, such as vibrational motions, take place at each chemical bond, like those between hydrogen and other atoms in the base pairs of DNA, with frequencies ranging from infrared to microwaves. In turn, these motions cause the charge on molecules to move, producing local electrical currents." (For much more information, see Kanev et al. 2012.)

Electrical pulses assist chromosome base pairs in message transmission. These pulses become intricately linked to the individual during fertilization and throughout the gestational period. (See Zhao and Zhan 2012 a and b for more on electric fields, replication, and cell division.) The frequency of electrical pulses between the double helices of the ancestors' chromosomes are thus passed from generation to generation—hence their offspring inherits radiant energy. (For more on ancestral energy, see Barreto 2019, 107.)

**The respiratory energy:** This is the respiratory kinetic energy of the movement and flow of air that the lungs project into the body. The respiratory system is both voluntary and involuntary, being the only one in the human body to have both characteristics. The vortex generated by such energy is air-related, not only regarding matter, but also to what hermetically relates to the mind and thought-forms. Because the respiratory system is the main way one absorbs etheric prana, depression or long-term sadness can cause problems in the lungs; similarly, the etheric bodies of individuals with lung problems need to take energy from their astral bodies to compensate for the lack of vital energy. (More about the metaphysics of lungs can be found in Sui 1992.)

**The food energy:** This is the chemical energy released when food calories are consumed by the digestive system. Alternatively, food energy may be understood as the chemical energy that animals gain via the process of cellular respiration.

There are two possible ways for food energy to be absorbed: aerobic respiration, in which food molecules undergo a chemical reaction with molecular oxygen, and anaerobic respiration, in which food molecules are reorganized without the presence of oxygen.

Besides offering chemical energy in the form of calories, food also gives the body information in the form of atoms. Along these lines, eating is a process where the physical body absorbs particles as the etheric body absorbs waves and therefore subtle information.

**The interpersonal energy:** This is the potential energy stored by the individual's compound field, generated by the auric fields of individuals physically and emotionally close to them. This type of energy is commonly called *field electrostatics,* where the set of charges between the mental and emotional fields of the individual and their companions generates a potential system of repulsion or attraction (For more on this, see Barreto 2019, 44).

Along these lines, the interaction with insects and other animals occurs, most of the time, via the energies mentioned. Insects and harmful bacteria in the house are attracted by energy imbalances arising from the place's disharmony. Despite the physical and natural reasons why an insect may appear, such as food crumbs, holes in the walls, and particularities of climate, it is indisputable that such disorder only unfolds on the physical plane when it is already a reality in the individual's etheric, mental, and emotional planes. What follows are descriptions of why several species appear and interact in the lives of humans. Where not otherwise noted, I received this information telepathically between the years 2018 and 2020.

## Bacteria

As Brazier (2019) explains, bacteria are single-cell organisms that are neither plants nor animals and that live both inside and outside organisms. They are thought to be the first beings to have appeared on Earth, around four billion years ago. Some bacteria produce oxygen, which played a vital role in creating the oxygen in Earth's atmosphere. Certain types of bacteria get their energy through consuming organic carbon. Most absorb dead organic material. Other types of bacteria are considered hazardous and conduits of diseases.

Types of bacteria vary, and they are commonly associated with transforming something into something else. O'Hara and Shanahan (2006) explain that bacteria in the digestive system break down nutrients, such as complex sugars, into forms the body can use.

In the Oxford Dictionary of Chemistry (6th ed.), the term *transmutation* is defined as "the transformation of one element into another by bombardment of nuclei with particles." In physics and chemistry, it means the changing of one element into another by radioactive decay, nuclear bombardment, or similar processes. Esotericism applies a parallel idea to that of those sciences. Based on both schools, energy transmutation can be understood to occur when an energy pattern is reversed to its opposite aspect (Savil 2015).

Metaphysically, bacteria are transmutative beings. That is, the etheric energy that collectively envelops them transmutes the elements of the environment. Hence, wherever bacteria are observed in the body or in the house—either the so-called beneficial bacteria found in the gut flora, or the hazardous ones in decaying flesh—there is the need to control stagnant or harmful emotions.

As bacteria convert elements and molecules into others, they can be assumed to have a transformative nature. Following this line of thought, the wavelength of their semiphysical aura coincides with their biological nature and is thus characterized by high frequencies. In this context, *high frequency* refers to a frequency capable of transmuting a holographic element. The colors violet and purple, for instance, depict the lowest wavelengths and the highest frequencies of the visible spectrum (Bruno et al. 2005), besides being the colors with the most photon energy, which is directly proportional to frequency. Beings with a transformative aura may have the function or capacity to bring a cycle to an end so that another can begin. Consequently, the bacteria that affect people and animals, either positively or negatively, absorb the etheric residues of organic or inorganic matter that are at the end of their lives.

The physical lives of cells are determined by a chemical state known as *equilibrium*. Equilibrium is a stage in which chemicals no longer tend to react over time (Lodish et al. 2000). In biology, it is well known that the life of a cell is based on the chemicals that exchange energy to keep each other from reaching equilibrium, which prevents the cells from dying. Thus, bacteria will only appear when equilibrium is evident.

Essentially, bacteria absorb stagnant energy and exude the prospect of new life. To eliminate harmful bacteria, such as the ones found in infections or wounds, or the ones that cause food poisoning, the ignored emotions in these parts of the body must be healed. The healing should be accompanied by the understanding that an emotion in that part of the body was stagnant or corrupted, and therefore at the end of its life. Likewise, wishing for the ending of an emotion may result in unconsciously attracting bacteria to one's organisms or house, thus having the bacteria do the renovation work, indicating an illness that is the somatization of that emotion.

### Insects

Insects are part of a collective system that is sustained by the imbalance of environments. They serve a noble purpose of balancing and stabilizing environments, either in the wilderness or in people's homes. Depending on the insect in question, the specific emotion in disharmony may be assessed.

### Ants

Ants emanate an energetic plasma that simulates a pheromone of pleasure and sweetness. These waves radiating from ants or anthill strings in the house indicate where such a plasma is missing. As ants exhale this pheromone of sweetness, they absorb the antagonists of sweetness and pleasure—in this case, bitterness and lack of interest.

It is worth taking into consideration that, similar to ants, most insects exhale and absorb such etheric particles and gases wherever they are, balancing emotionally affected environments. The use of insecticides does not solve the problem; quite the contrary, it evidences a disregard for life.

Simple attitudes may divert ants from the house. A neatly swept and organized home can suffice. Moreover, pots with flowers and cheerful pictures on the walls have a colossal impact on individuals' psyches. Fresh bedding and open windows are excellent to keep ants at bay. Lastly, broken objects should be discarded. Once the home is etherically "sweet," it will turn bitter for ants, which will in turn then leave.

## Cockroaches

Cockroaches exude a semiphysical plasma of conservation while absorbing the etheric gases of disgust. Wherever a cockroach can be found, there resides a need for conservation, either physical or moral. These insects are a sign that self-preservation and self-protection are needed, as it is clear that there is something the individual wishes to eliminate from their life.

The fact that cockroaches absorb the dense energies of the environment, such as those of aversion, indicates that these insects spontaneously act in the dissociation of etheric putrid gases. Just as the elementals of nature filter the subtlest ethers, cockroaches filter the densest ethers. In this way, they involuntarily warn that extra care must be taken. These alerts are not exclusively for humans, but also for other animals in the environment, who instinctively perceive them. In fact nature is balanced with the help of all insects, animals, and plants that are part of it.

The persistent killing of cockroaches will not solve the problem of their presence. On the contrary, others will appear to continue the motion of exuding and absorbing. Thus, it is recommended that the individual affected by an infestation alter their low mental and emotional patterns to patterns of a higher frequency.

Acceptance of the space in which an individual lives is crucially necessary, as is the understanding that other individuals do not invade anyone's space. It is also important that individuals themselves do not unconsciously auto-project judgment and disgust of the world.

## Spiders

Spiders only appear in places where the energies of professional work are not being exercised. This may involve stagnant thoughts of doubt, stunted ideals, and undetectable desire to invest in a career. Spiders may also suggest mental or physical lethargy.

When spiders appear, they occupy the precise areas where that professional labor energy is scarcely found. Spiders absorb stagnation and exude etheric plasma similar to the planning of work that requires physical or intellectual effort. Undoubtedly, owning a house in the countryside or an apartment on the fiftieth floor will be decisive for the appearance of spiders; nevertheless, the consciousness that inhabits a house in the woods and the consciousness that lives on the fiftieth floor of a skyscraper think rather differently from each other about professional success.

The spiders' webs will only be made on surfaces lacking professional energy; therefore, books covered in webs must be read, and ceilings or walls camouflaged with them demand the repositioning of furniture or for the room to be redecorated.

In the case of a spider infestation, investing in a course or studies should be considered. Additionally, reading, planning, and work from home improve the issue.

In nature, spiders play a role in stimulating other insects and small port animals to physiologically develop survival skills.

## Butterflies

Butterflies are surrounded by etheric currents that vibrate at frequencies that closely resemble thought-forms. Therefore, butterflies can be observed in places where thought-forms are abundant, even in the wilderness.

Exteriorized thoughts are composed of a stream of subtle particles and waves, while thought-forms are constituted by the etheric solidification of much more complex thoughts.

Thought-forms are also the main conductor of the energy marks of a particular place, which was theorized as the *morphogenetic field*.

Morphogenetic fields indicate that, biologically, all populations are informed by consciousness fields previously irradiated by other beings of the same species. A morphogenetic field is, therefore, a memory field that all species move through, think by, and behave in relation to correspondingly (Sheldrake 2011).

Butterflies are enveloped in a frequency close to that of thought-forms, hence in certain circumstances, they will interact or behave according to them. That is, they may be influenced by the thought-forms of the environment, and may influence them.

Metaphysically, butterflies absorb the energies that spread in all directions simultaneously, while exhaling waves that redirect these thoughts. Depending on the energetic eminence of the thought-forms, it may be that a butterfly is naturally attracted near to where the thought-form is, to experience more of that energy familiar to the species.

It is also important to emphasize that only in abnormal circumstances will butterflies interact with the thought-forms of humans, such as by landing on a certain book when there is an examination to be taken, or landing on a photo frame while one is thinking deeply about who is in the image, or perhaps landing on top of the head at the time of prayer, or even landing on a bunch of keys when a decision is made. Insects of all types appear only when the etheric vibration of places makes this possible.

As discussed, insects are mainly governed by a collective etheric plasma. That is, a group of insects behaves and evolves as if it were part of an entire soul. This collective "soul" travels in the physical and semiphysical world, absorbing and exhaling ethers invisible to physical eyes. This indicates how each insect on Earth is needed to balance the planet's frequency.

It is advantageous to talk to the insects in the case of an infestation. Communication is not properly done through words, but through the vibrational field of the human and the vibrational field of insects. As nature establishes the equilibrium of forces, the vibrational fields of both will attempt to achieve that balance. Consequently, both humans and insects will be urged to change, no longer needing each other's presence to achieve the equilibrium of forces in nature.

## The Etheric Nature of Insects

As mentioned, ants ooze a pheromone of sweetness. They are beings that have an etheric constitution at the frequency of love, which includes other ideas such as kindness, diplomacy, and harmonic beauty. These frequency bands are different frequencies of Source, and paralleling Source with a rainbow, each color vibrates in a different oscillation and amplitude, red having the longest range, and violet the shortest.

Each of these vibrating sections, exemplified as colors of a rainbow, are different shades of the same Source or God. Hence, the seven basic frequencies can be denominated as shown in the table. (These colors represent a descriptive example and may not fully relate to chromotherapy methods or chakras and their hues.)

| Color | Characteristic |
|-------|----------------|
| White | Faith |
| Violet | Evolution |
| Blue | Generation |
| Cyan | Law |
| Green | Knowledge |
| Yellow | Love |
| Red | Justice |

Within these basic frequencies, others are also expressed as derivations of the initial frequencies. As examples: movement, which derives from law; peace, which derives from faith; work, which derives from knowledge; kindness, which derives from love.

The ether that is radiated onto ants stems from the frequency of the Source related to love. Although ants have been generated in the wave of love as their patrons, they underwent an extensive evolutionary journey before becoming ants. They may have been mineral plasma, unicellular beings, or other insects before reaching their current form as ants. All were commonly sustained in their evolution by the frequency of love.

As ants collectively migrate and reincarnate as individualized animals, it is pivotal to reiterate that an individual animal with an Atman will not equal the number of insects in a colony. For example, a colony of 2,800 ants does not mean 2,800 future individualized animals. Most likely, one Atman radiates to all ants in the colony, which implies that groups of ants reincarnate as one single individualized animal. As such, ants are likely to migrate to individual animals whose Atman derives from the frequency of love.

All animals, including insects, are beings that were generated by one of the specific waves of creation. Source creates all matter from distinct bands of frequency, which gives unique characteristics to each element created.

Assuming that ants could navigate across other realms while keeping their essence when turning into beings of another species, they would likely be rose quartz crystals if they entered the mineral kingdom. They would be roses or passion fruit flowers if they were to become part of the *plantae* kingdom. Along these lines, they would find themselves as chickens, peacocks, herons, or storks if they were to initiate their lives in this class of animals. The proposed correlation does not suggest that ants etherically move to the beings mentioned; rather, it is intended to aid in comprehending how the same divine attributes are manifest in each respective kingdom.

Such compatibility is defined concerning the frequency from each of the aforementioned beings descended. The frequency of love notably associates ants, rose quartz, roses, and chickens into a group that shares a spiritual gene of love within their Atmans and their astral and etheric encapsulations. All animals, including insects, are beings that were generated by one of the qualities of Source.

Although various bees are linked to honey, these insects have had their divine sparks detached from the waves of Generation, or more precisely, Motherhood. Their "patron" Atmans, that is, the Atmans that are to animate individual beings, emerge from the power of divine generation; however, each being in the universe acquires other frequency enhancements during its evolution, either as a collective group or as an individual. The Atman, or divine spark, remains unaffected, although the capsules in the form of other bodies temporarily grant nuances of other divine aspects. Thus, bees emerged from the frequency of

Generation, simultaneously supported by the frequency of knowledge, or more explicitly, the frequencies of work and labor. The spiritual journey of bees commenced on the planet Venus (Steiner 1923). There, as collective spirits behaving and gathering experience as if the group were one soul, they were incarnated in a substantially more subtle plane than the third dimension experienced on Earth. Hence, life on Venus is categorically impossible for animals or plants of the Earth. However, according to Kardec (1857) not every spirit in the universe experiences "incarnation" in the physical third dimension, but may instead, or in addition, experience incarnation in other dimensions either subtler or denser than that experienced on Earth.

### Mice and Rats

Mice, as well as rats, are animals already constituted with a fully structured astral body; however, they are still thoroughly connected to other nearby rats and mice spiritually, as if they were a group of a singular soul.

The energy that sustains rats and mice, varying in intensity between the two groups, is one of the most unstable in the animal world. Rats and mice are capable of feeling the frequency variations more sharply than the vast majority of animals, even more so than cats or dogs.

The etheric reality of rats does not diverge from this line of thought. Rats possess etheric energy that is constantly changing in frequency. They are animals that both interact with benevolent, organized, and enlightened frequencies, as well as with the densest, most chaotic, and darkest frequencies. These qualities can be observed from a purely physical point of view, as mice are found both in putrid sewer holes and in clean and airy rooms in houses, modern offices, and spacious churches.

Mice appear in areas where etheric waves conflict, exhibiting a variety of frequencies. Although mice have extensive adaptive skills to dwell in different frequency layers, they are attracted to places where such frequency conflict is constant.

Incontestably, there are materialistic reasons why rats and mice appear, which are key to determining such an occurrence in the physical world. However, metaphysical interpretation offers the primary motivation why matter and physical beings behave in such ways. The materialistic reasons are based on observational agents, whereas a metaphysical explanation focuses on the astral factors behind reality as it is experienced.

As an example, the materialistic reasons why mice infest a house could be gaps in the walls or food crumbs on the floor. This, however, fails to explain why an individual would live in a house with gaps in the walls or why they would have floors covered with food crumbs.

In order to keep rats and mice away from home, the conflicting frequencies in the environment must be ceased. These conflicts in certain sites are generated by individuals whose emotional discrepancies are continual; for example, a person praying devoutly in the morning who later at night has an altercation at the same place, or the individual who beautifully makes a bed while leaving the chest of drawers completely disorganized, or even someone who lives in chaos at home, but is serene and organized on the street or at work.

These conflicting energies can be generated by either emotional or physical causes, linked to habits. Rats and mice only appear when there is chaos and conflict generated by the individuals who spend considerable amounts of time in those places. Hence, rats and mice will not feel at ease in places with no variation of frequency, as they may feel maladjusted.

The more calamitous or nefarious the energies, the more prone to

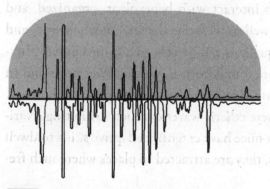

Fig. 3.1. Upon encountering a human's conflicting thoughts, the etheric waves of rats and mice involuntarily compensate for the peaks and valleys, aiming for an equilibrium. (Illustration example for comparison only). Illustration by David Barreto.

■ **likelihood of the presence of mice and rats**

□ **conflicting thought waves**

rats a place would be. The more superficial or flippant the energies, the more prone to mice a place would be.

It is therefore not suggested that traps be used. Killing rats to get rid of them is paradoxical, since these animals are unconsciously attracted to repairing the energy imbalance of the environment. In addition, the holes and gaps in the walls must be sealed and all areas must be cleaned regularly. Ultimately, positive thoughts, emotions, and habits that are aligned with each other must be cultivated.

## Horses

Considering several animals with a pineal gland—more specifically cats, owls, and horses—it is noticed that much of their behavior is established by magnetic signals received by the antenna gland.

Horses are among the animals that have the most developed pineal gland, from an extraphysical point of view. Most horses have premonitions and a keen intuition, and they may, in certain circumstances, witness disembodied spirits. Horses are also one of the closest spirits to migrate to a viable hominid realm.

## Cats

Cats sleep most of the day because at night they filter out harmful energy from the environment. Physiologically, they save energy during the day, hence after sunset and before sunrise is the time when they are most active. This pattern demonstrates the compatibility between physiological and extraphysical behaviors.

The biological and instinctual reasons for such behavior are important, but the extraphysical argument is the primal reason cats' physical bodies developed in this way. The part of the house where cats lie is presumably the place where the most energetic attention is needed.

Cats' eyes are also powerful vortices of subtle energy, and their magnetism is not due merely to their physical attractiveness. The electromagnetic field generated by the feline pineal gland, especially that of the domestic cat, is extraordinarily sensitive to the macrocosmic and interpersonal energies of their owners. Cats can detect energy shifts in field networks, both from the environment and from other beings.

Additionally, their pineal glands can channel the frequency of thoughts of humans, sensing whether those humans have an innocent or corrupt intention toward them. In the etheric dimensions, they may perceive regions where there is a lack of vital energy, and so involuntarily commence a process of etheric filtration, where they sleep close to these areas to promote their revitalization.

Under such circumstances, cats cleanse and demagnetize holographic toxins in their owners' electromagnetic fields. Cats are comparable to clear crystals, as they also stimulate mental clarity in their owners.

The more energetically imbalanced the house or the owner's aura, the more corrosive energy the cat may absorb, which perhaps leaves the cat prone to a compromised state of health.

Between three and four thirty in the morning cats most transmute energy, as it is the part of the day when less vital energy flows in the environment. It is hence recommended that cats are allowed to sleep at any given time they require and that appropriate attention should be given to the area where a cat chooses to sleep, ensuring its physical and energetic cleanliness.

### Owls and Eagles
Owls and eagles are related to night and day, respectively. That is, while the former's instincts will thrive at night, the latter's nature excels during the day. Interestingly, owls have perfect night vision (Martin 1982), while eagles have incredible eyesight during the day. The eyes of eagles are large compared to the size of their heads, as the posterior corner of their eyeball exhibits a flatter and larger back wall than that of humans' eyes. Such a contour permits them wider view angles. The eyesight of eagles is five times more accurate than that of humans; moreover, they can detect ultraviolet light, which human eyes cannot (Wolchover 2012).

Their astute capabilities resonate with their own astral aspects. In other words, eagles have such physical capabilities as a result of the divine nature of their essence. These two birds carry a generous amount of apatite crystals in their pineal glands, which have their atoms' elementary particles strictly arranged in peculiar shapes, allowing the antenna gland to easily tune in to the subtle planes of the intellect (Baconnier and Lang 2004; though not mentioning birds, the constitution of their pineal glands differs little, as per Pal et al. 2013).

The plane of the intellect, which is a distinct layer derived from other dimensions, allows knowledge and facts to be considered from different angles in synchronicity.

Both owls and eagles act their etheric energies on physical renewal and rebirth. Eagles and owls are constantly renewing their physical bodies. When eagles damage a beak or talon, because these appendages are made of keratin they are able to grow back (McGlashen 2019). They also hone, sharpen, and trim their own beaks.

Owls couple intellect with intuition. Their impeccable night vision and their nonphysical bodies are highly efficient at comprehending what implicit events mean.

## Pigeons

The sounds emitted by animals such as dolphins and pigeons drift into phonon waves, which are quasiparticles associated with sound, just as the photons are associated with light. Both pigeons and dolphins can balance entangled damaging etheric currents.

All sorts of pigeons act on the mental cleansing of egregores,* which is the spiritual force created by the sum of the collective mental and emotional energies of a group. Pigeons, therefore, influence the respiratory energy of individuals as well as undo group mental confusion, especially in places where there is considerable transit or influx of people.

Pigeons have a sense called magnetoreception, which allows them to detect Earth's magnetic field to perceive direction, altitude, or location. Physiologically, pigeons' magnetic receptors allow them to navi-

---

*An egregore is the spiritual energy resulting from the sum of thoughts of a group. Often, an egregore can also be considered as a group of spirits with a common purpose.

gate, which includes the ability, in homing pigeons, to return to their homes using the capacity to sense the Earth's magnetic field and other cues to orient themselves. (For more about pigeons, see Wiltschko and Wiltschko 2012, Walcott 1996, and Gould 1984.)

Curiously, when assessing the more subtle properties of electromagnetism sensing, pigeons emit sounds in an attempt to share information on "what to do" or "where to go." Their sound chain intercepts the intertwined phonon waves present in the area, thus dissipating the local mental nodes. The mental nodes of any humans nearby are also favorably influenced by the passing sounds.

## Dolphins

Pigeons are animals of the air, while dolphins live in water. This difference characterizes pigeons as healers of the mind, while dolphins are the healers of emotions.

According to marine life researcher John Lilly (1961), dolphins use their sonar system of clicks, whistles, and trills to produce echoes in order to detect the details of objects hundreds of meters away under water, which is nearly five times faster at conducting sound waves than air. The phenomenon described by Lilly was pioneered by Kenneth S. Norris (1961), a marine mammal biologist who discovered echolocation among cetaceans. Echolocation is a method of localization that relies on sound waves bouncing off objects. The use of echolocation to determine the density of objects is done when the animal emits a sound and receives its echo, therefore creating acoustics and 3D shapes in their head and thereby calculating their density.

Metaphysically, the sounds of dolphins perform an involuntary cleansing on depressive emotions that are entangled. Their sounds dispel sadness in the emotional bodies of individuals, and the scenes that caused the trauma, as well as all its traces in one's mental body, may also be dissipated by the dolphin itself, although the latter is performed secondarily, on rare occasions.

The echoing can trigger entangled and deeply anchored emotions in the subconscious, bringing them to the surface to finally be dismantled.

The healing effects of listening to dolphin sounds is indeed a gradual and relatively slow process; nevertheless, it is effective as a side therapy for depressed individuals, those who may have lost a loved one, and those who struggle to find a purpose in life.

Several spiritual rescue groups have used such natural sounds to treat the spirits of depressive suicidal individuals, such is the healing power of that vibration. Rescue teams that are organized by enlightened spirits generally need an ever-so-slightly denser form of energy when managing cases where the patient is still profoundly attached to earthly conditioning. Thus, these teams gather the rescued individuals to accompany them to areas of the sea where there are many dolphins, whose sounds and vibrations help dissipate the agonies and traumas of the afflicted.

In other dimensions, the sounds emitted by dolphins reverberate inside the object or throughout the individual's subtle bodies, so the dolphin may recognize what sort of emotional "filling" is there by their echoes. Thus, if they perceive it to be unfavorable, as in depressive memories, they may dissolve it.

## Whales

The sounds of whales refer to feminine polarity vibrations capable of disintegrating unconscious traumas related to guilt, fear, and shame, thus enabling these destructive emotions to be assessed and healed. It is no coincidence that numerous cultures associate the relationship between whales and oceans with the subconscious mind.

In the Old Testament's book of Jonah, Jonah disobeys the orders of God and, as a result, becomes depressed and distressed for not following what the Creator had asked him to do. Then, on being thrown into the sea, Jonah is swallowed by a whale (or "big fish"), staying three days in the animal's belly. Jonah says the three days were pure fear, as he was in the most abysmal place in the world. However, when he asked for forgiveness, God orders the big fish to vomit Jonah.

Coincidence or not, the astral implications of whale sounds are directly connected to overcoming traumas and guilt. Perhaps when these animals evolve to a more intellectual realm, they may acquire the ability to assist the emotionally traumatized.

It is well known that many people find the sounds emitted by whales to be calming and soothing, perhaps unconsciously leading listeners to slow down their breathing, which may aid in relieving anxiety episodes. Metaphysically, these healing sounds are interpreted as maternal, non-threatening sounds, which gently agitate the depths of one's lower mental body's crystallized traumas that might have developed throughout upbringing. This results in a sedative sensation, thereby ameliorating the processes of eliminating such agonies. It is worth noting that these sounds, recorded on digital devices, can be used in the treatment of animals victimized by trauma and physical shock.

### Bats

Despite being extensively linked to witchcraft, legends of vampires and general evil, bats are a group of animals that, metaphysically, are identified with dissipating mental stagnation. Circumstantially associated with the macabre, both bats and spiders are beings that act where and when the lack of vigorous mental activity is perceptible.

Both animals are correlated with the qualities of the element air, which contains intellect, thoughts, imagination, and ideas. Spiders, however, are conduits of intellectualized labor, whereas bats are conduits of intellectualized courage—that is, courage based on evidence and facts.

Bats are also known for their impressive echolocation capability, which resembles that of dolphins (Lima and O'Keefe 2013). Bat's echolocation calls range in frequency from 14,000 to over 100,000 Hz. Bats emit much longer signals than dolphins, as well as more varied ones. These nocturnal animals interpret data much quicker than most species with echolocation, which grants them the power to simultaneously aim on several different targets when after insects or other animals.

This natural etheric trait of bats is beneficial to all mammals afraid of taking action, as the bats' whistle may rip dense nodes of etheric forms that resemble apprehension and suspicion in frequency and color.

Hence, a stroll in a dark forest may dismantle more fears than just that of the dark forest itself.

Antagonistically, the archetype of bats has been associated with less beneficial characteristics, such was the correlation between these creatures with evil and dark forces throughout the centuries, in virtually all cultures. Thus, it is important to understand that bats, like spiders, are divine components of evolution and have nothing to do with harmful magic or any demonological connotations.

## Sparrows and Canaries

Birds such as sparrows are sensitive to signals from mental currents. They adapt to these subtle signals, behaving differently due to interaction with the thought-forms of humans and other mammals.

Like sparrows, canaries are sensitive to mental images, and they normally sing more than the former. Both sorts of birds, as well as budgies, lovebirds, and cockatiels, do not only sing as a result of thought-forms, as a warning, or as supernatural hypothesizing; singing is a natural and instinctual trait for them. Nevertheless, the abnormal or unusual behavior of a bird may perhaps indicate that a friendly spirit is attempting to communicate, although these occurrences are exceptionally rare.

In metaphysics, sparrows stimulate focus, not only in humans but in other animals too. It is convenient to remember that all animal extraphysical activity has distinct effects on both humans and other animals. Canaries denote favorable ideas, unraveling conflicting thoughts. In the wild, canaries boost local mental activity, regardless of the presence of humans. Mental activity, therefore, should not be understood as an exclusively human faculty.

## Dogs

Dogs have a tremendous capacity for loving unconditionally. The center of a dog's electromagnetic field is one of the largest in the animal kingdom, thus the purification of degrading and depressing emotions in the environment is efficiently accomplished by the strong currents coming from the canine heart chakras. Their powerful vortex influences humans on the grounds of interpersonal energies. Dogs are among a limited number of animals able to have such effects, invariably nourishing to the etheric bodies of humans. This influence occurs as the dogs "soften the individuals' hearts" by dissolving resentments, while pleasantly filling energy gaps caused by the rigidity of adult life.

Although granted intellectual traits, dogs are primarily developing emotional skills in their incarnations.

Dogs are uncommonly synergetic—that is, they smell energy and may even see it in some cases. They prudently distinguish positive energy from malefic energy, hence they regularly sleep in the cleanest areas in the house, unless told not to do so.

Metaphysically, hair or fur relates to one's superiors—one's power figure, owner, or boss. If envious forces are projected against an individual, their dog may develop hair problems, as an involuntary mechanism of protecting the human they honor.

Despite what some may assume, dogs are neither foolish nor emptyheaded for repeatedly "coming back wagging their tails" to those who were cruel to them. This is due to their ability to easily forgive. In such a way, dogs involuntarily help humans to learn to forgive, reflecting purity in its highest degree. Their astral bodies are fully formed, but still, they will not hold indignation or wrath against others. They do not need to redeem karma debts, only learn new experiences.

The nonphysical version of the dog's thymus gland, which is the subtle center of love, next to the heart, works energetically identically to the thymus glands found in humans.

Dogs expand benevolent energies, whereas cats transmute malefic ones. The reason cats transmute and dogs expand energies is due to the direction in which their electromagnetic currents move. The electromagnetic field of cats is centripetal, while that of the dog is centrifugal. This means that cats absorb the negative energy, transmute it within themselves and thereupon return it to the environment. Dogs, alternatively, generate positive energy within themselves, redistributing it.

The reason cats will not absorb every single type of energy except the harmful ones is plainly due to the frequency in which the energies vibrate. Cats' electromagnetic fields, which are negative in polarization, will only interlace with positive currents—that is, the environment's negative energies. They thus "drag" these sorts of energies to the center of their electromagnetic field, where transmutation occurs. The transmutation performed by a cat is a process where particles and waves are spun to the opposite direction of natural spin.

Dogs, on the other hand, have their fields performing in an expansive—that is, centrifugal—way. Therefore, they do not draw energy, as the movement is naturally from the inside out. However, dogs become emotionally attached to their owners and, consequently, they feel and connect to their auras. As such, these animals may somatize in themselves energetic imbalances from the human. Somatization, in this case, is the surge of diseases in the physical body due to imbalances found in one's most subtle bodies, such as the etheric and the astral bodies.

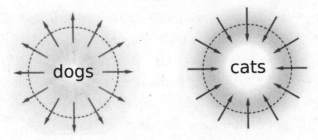

Fig 3.2. Dogs exude beneficial ethers, whereas cats absorb malefic ethers. Illustration by David Barreto.

Domesticated animals commonly radiate more beneficial ethers than the humans they share the house with, as they normally lack negative thoughts and malicious behavior. Therefore, episodes of energetic compensation may occur when they involuntarily donate their energies to the human auric fields, hence developing the very diseases meant to afflict the human.

Finally, the energy of all animals, either small insects or intelligent mammals, will inevitably interact with the energies of other animals and of humans. Mediumistic abilities in humans may also be nothing but fundamental characteristics inherent in several animals.

# PART 2

· · · · · · · · · ·

# IMPACTS OF HUMAN ACTIVITIES ON ANIMALS' SPIRITUAL JOURNEYS

# 4 Spiritual Repercussions of Eating Meat

The spiritual and energetic repercussions of eating meat must be understood as the reaction one's subtle body displays after the ingestion of meat* or other etherically toxic foods of animal origin, such as dairy products.

The totality of the human being, as an incarnated spirit, is composed of seven main bodies. They are the Physical; the Etheric; the Astral; the Lower Mental; the Upper Mental; the Buddhic (or Buddhi); and the Atman body. Through some of these bodies and meridians, several types of energy are distributed. Meridians carry qi (also spelled chi) or prana from and to the physical body. These energy canals also conduct other categories of energy that travel through the physical organs, tissues, and liquids to and from the etheric body and the astral body. They are the macrocosmic energy, ancestral energy, respiratory energy, food energy, and interpersonal energy.

With reference to the bodies and types of energy, meat is to be assessed for its etheric components, as well as "where" and "how" these energies reverberate in the human body.

---

*The following chapter will exclusively discuss meat. However, some of the concepts discussed here may be applied to other foods and by-products or services resulting from animal exploitation, such as the use of skins, furs, feathers, and bones.

## MEAT AND ANTIMATTER

Along with a physical body, animals are endowed with an etheric body that provides them with energy at the same time as it serves as a glue between their physical bodies and their astral bodies. Their astral bodies, like those of humans, are the duplicates of their physical bodies in the astral dimension.

The emotions of sentient beings are typically stored in their astral bodies. When negative, these emotions are carriers of what can be understood as a sort of antimatter in the subtle planes.

Antimatter is one of the main components of the commonly named "negative energy." According to modern physicist Paul Dirac (1965, 320–25), a particle of matter and a particle of antimatter both have the same mass, but the electrical charge of antimatter is generally opposite that of ordinary matter, as exemplified in the case of the electron and positron or the proton and antiproton.

A clairvoyant medium can observe nonphysical toxins in the auras of individuals, either as particles or as waves. These peculiar reversed particles in the aura signify for the individual an energetic deficiency caused by the stagnation of vital flow and the accumulation of astral detritus.

Naturally, the physical body is composed of matter; however, the etheric body is constituted of subtle matter, which can be understood as regular matter, but natural to another dimension. Everything in the physical dimension is composed of matter, made up of electrons, quarks, and other elementary particles. Every particle (and antiparticle) is fundamentally an excitation in all-permeating quantum fields.

Harrison (2000) explains that when particles and antiparticles meet, they annihilate each other, releasing energy in the form of photons (light) and other particles, such as gamma rays and neutrinos. The energy of the annihilated particles can cause ionization by detaching electrons from atoms or molecules, reducing the size of the electromagnetic field. It is important to note that the energy released from the annihilation of particles and antiparticles is not solely in the form of ionizing radiation. Some of the energy can also appear in the form of nonionizing radiation, such as low-energy photons.

If the surrounding subtle matter, or holographic matter, is present during annihilation, the energy content of this radiation will be absorbed and converted into other forms of energy, such as destructive heat or light, proportional to the total mass, per the well-known mass-energy equivalence equation, $E = mc^2$.

Overall, subtle antimatter annihilates subtle matter. Drawing a parallel to etheric toxins, it can be assumed that these semiphysical particles somatize as illness; that is, they manifest as ailments on the etheric body and thus negatively affect the physical body. It is also crucial to emphasize that the etheric toxins found in the subtle bodies are semiphysical particles.

Every particle or quantum body can be described as either a particle or a wave. According to the concept of wave-particle duality, its description depends on how it is observed and measured. Thus, along with the ingestion of meat, there is the unavoidable ingestion of its electromagnetic wave, which contains information on how that flesh was generated. The information is presented as distortions caused by etheric toxins, which disfigure the wave frequency patterns. As the eaten meat becomes part of the physical body, the electromagnetic wave that constitutes it will become part of the individual's electromagnetic field.

By attracting what can be understood as antimatter to its own etheric body through ingestion, the individual causes the destruction of holographic matter as well as the destruction of the attracted antimatter—that is, they annihilate each other, causing loss of vital fluids in a region of the body where the energy canals were blocked or in the entire physical body altogether. This mutual annihilation leads to the release and loss of holographic photons and neutrinos in the etheric body. Therefore, lacking a natural flow of vital energy, the physical body will present epigenetic and emotional abnormalities. (See Lipton 2005.)

In a similar vein, the consumption of antimatter found in meat in the form of waves perforates the etheric body of those who consume it, since antimatter annihilates matter, which is in its etheric form a hologram. Etheric matter, or ethereal matter, is matter in its embryonic stage. It commonly condenses as physical matter, to make part of one's physical body.

Overall, antimatter invariably appears on the subtle bodies before manifesting as disease in the physical body.

Although it is presumed that meat offers one of the five types of subtle energy, it is imperative to add that the molecular and atomic constitution of any foods also indicates the quality of energy being transmitted and absorbed, not just the calories.

The pains that an animal experiences at the very moment of death, or the panic that precedes it, leaves scarring marks on its etheric body. The etheric body is the subtle body that vitalizes the physical body with vital fluids. This means that these dreadful feelings, which reside at low vibration frequencies, permeate the animal's flesh, as well as the rest of their physical bodies.

In these circumstances, there is no "energy cleansing" that could potentially liberate the meat from such energies, since the physical molecules of the meat have been generated or redefined at a molecular level, under such low vibrations.

The terror and pain during their deaths are not the only moments that affect their physical bodies on this level. Confinement and incapability of expressing their natural instincts also influences their subtle bodies, including the lower and upper mental bodies. Calves that are taken from their mothers, seconds after birth; chickens that never enjoy spreading their wings; pigs that will never touch the natural ground or see a ray of sunlight during their lives—all this suffering contributes to shaping how each molecule of their meats will be generated at the subatomic level.

*Elementars** are static beings shaped by the repeated emotions of

---

*Elementars can be understood as an artificial elemental, and for didactic reasons, this work will refer to artificial elementals as *elementars*. Elementars are energies shaped in the astral dimension, whereas elementals are, in most cases, prototypes of the souls of animals or other beings who dwell in certain astral and etheric layers of nature. *Elementars*, along these lines, is a coined term from *elementals*—however, the former are not living beings, while the latter are.

incarnated sentient beings. They are the result of beliefs and thoughts sustained by strong feelings. The elementars are intensified holograms, which have no life of their own, but appear to exercise some function in the astral world. Under constant terror, animals will involuntarily fabricate elementars, which may remain clung to their physical bodies and, so, to their flesh.

The vast majority of animals lined up to be slaughtered create a form of an etheric shield around themselves as a means of protection. Unfortunately, this shield is nothing more than a holographic projection of their energies. These shields are described as elementars.

Upon being killed, the astral bodies of those animals separate from their toxic shields. However, their corpses still retain attachments to those etheric remains. Generally, elementars produced in life act as a toxic layer over those who produce them, which would serve to deter the enemy—those who pose a threat to the individual producing such energy shields. When eating meat, there is a possibility of consuming its allocated elementars.

## PSYCHOSOMATIC COMPLICATIONS

Upon eating meat, the transfer of vital fluids from subtle bodies to the physical body is reduced as a result of blockages caused by the low amplitude of frequency in the meat, which in turn prevents energy in the subtle body from moving smoothly.

The emotional body of an individual who has eaten meat will naturally assimilate the feelings attached to the meat. This may motivate psychosomatic illnesses, which occur when the mind and emotions generate a physical disease in the body itself, in a forced activity to purge those feelings.

The animal's feelings attached to the flesh could be classified by the amount of accumulated astral antimatter in it, in addition to other particles derived from their thought-forms and elementars.

It is over the solar plexus that the navel chakra, or *Manipura,* is situated. In humans, the solar plexus's* etheric energy fundamentally

---

*The solar plexus, also called celiac plexus, is not a chakra, but a physiological area in the human body. It is called solar plexus due to its radiating nerves, which resemble the sun.

exists to provide humans with an etheric shield, as well as functioning as a natural antenna to allow better perception from the environment. However, after eating meat, a considerable amount of etheric energy from that energy vortex is redirected to aid digestion. Therefore, the individual's aura is momentarily compromised by the lack of etheric energy, which leaves it noticeably dispersed and subject to alien energies. For this reason, among others, various spiritual workers and mediums abstain from eating meat on the days when they should work with their subtle energies.

Humans have approximately 30 trillion cells in their body (Sender, Fuchs, and Milo 2016), and within each cell there is a prototype system fairly similar to other large systems that comprise the human body in its entirety: a respiratory system, a digestive system, an excretory system, an endocrine system, a nervous system, a reproductive system, and an immune system, as well as a nucleus, in which the entire genetic code is found.

In cell biology, it was believed that the nucleus of the cell would be associated with its "brain," an organ responsible for dictating how and when any voluntary or involuntary task is to be performed. This is still the case, as cells need a nucleus to divide themselves in order to replicate.

Nevertheless, it was discovered that the cells continued to live for approximately 60 days and still performed most tasks after they had their nuclei removed. For this reason, the nucleus is not the only system to control the cell, though it remains their primary control source. The research also concluded that the membranes of cells were able to read external signals from the environment and, therefore, they were able to send these signals to proteins, telling them what to do. Thus, the membrane, not just the nucleus, played a role in telling proteins how to behave. (See Lipton 2005 as well as Nijhout 1990 and 1991.)

The signals perceived by the cell's membrane are of electric, chemical and electromagnetic nature. They are commonly associated with emotions, being transported by, but not limited to, neuropeptides and blood plasma. Whenever a thought occurs, biological reactions follow, which indicates physical feedback. This implies that thoughts, via electrical and chemical derivatives, generate physical events. Along these lines, it is understood that the thoughts of the mind influence the physical brain at the pace that the brain influences the mind.

Lipton's 2005 research explains the action of thoughts on organic cells: whenever a thought occurs, an emotion follows. The emotion, physiologically perceived, is generated by neurotransmitters in the synapses. Lipton's research has found that in the hypothalamus, these neurotransmitters join small chains of amino acids, producing neuro-peptides. These neuropeptides act as activating hormones that spread through the blood. Once all cells have receptors for this neural chemis-try, the peptides bind to the cell membrane, activating or deactivating genetic activity.

The behavior of cells can be influenced by the quality of neuropep-tides, which modulate gene expression through epigenetic mechanisms. Such a mechanism affects how cells work, altering the production of protein, changing inflammatory response, and modulating immuno-logical behavior.

Thoughts that start as immaterial occurrences become material phenomena in the body; likewise, cerebral automatism generates an idea, and that is reflected organically.

In conclusion, the cell's response to the environment is critically dependent on both its nucleus along with what its membrane may per-ceive in its environment. This suggests that cells do behave and con-sequently may mutate as a result of their physiologic surroundings, regardless of what their DNA may carry.

Correspondingly, the pain and emotions that animals experience during their lives may impact the behavior and development of their cells, which certainly include their flesh.

When the individual lives in chaos, surrounded by wrinkled clothes on the floor and dirty bed linens, the attraction of more astral chaos occurs, which may inevitably drift to the vicinity's physical plane. The same thing happens with regard to accumulated dust and the general rubbish that accumulates. Nevertheless, it is in the fridge and cupboards where such putrid condensation may attract the most chaotic varieties of astral waste.

Foods that are bought but not eaten, and that expire and rot, generate a decaying quality of gases that spread into other foods and into the corners of one's home. These etheric gases block the flow of energy, causing mold, infiltration, and insect infestations. This may even affect money flow and general health.

Even though they may be stored in the freezer or in vacuum-sealed tins, or even may not be expired, meats in the cupboard and fridge go through a putrefaction process in the etheric dimensions, emitting a sort of deep taupe color fume, typically associated with astral worms. Animal fur and leather also undergo etheric putrefaction. Once in contact with the individual who wears it, the material may absorb, albeit moderately, some of the wearer's auric particles to etherically decompose in its totality.

## THE ETHERIC GENERATION OF FLESH

In quantum field theory, the quantum vacuum state is the quantum state with the lowest possible energy. Though it does not contain physical particles, it is also not empty space. According to Dittrich and Gies (2000), the vacuum state is not truly empty but instead contains fleeting electromagnetic waves and particles that continually emerge and disappear from existence. The Higgs field, which is a quantum field, exists everywhere in the physical universe. Particles that interact with the Higgs field gain mass from it, known as the Higgs effect. Gaining mass results in the slowing down of the particle, which also loses the ability to travel at the speed of light. Additionally, because particles would have no mass to attract other particles, there would be no gravity, and particles would remain traveling at the speed of light.

The Higgs effect transfers mass or energy to any particle. However, light that passes through it gains energy, but not mass, as its waveform does not have mass, while its particle form constantly travels at light speed. Once the field has given mass to a formerly massless particle, the particle in question will slow down and become "heavy," which may be understood as "materialized."

It is generally accepted that there is only one field in the universe, the electromagnetic quantum vacuum. However, other fields are accepted to be parts of it, such as the Higgs field and the gravitational field. In this context, the Higgs field is the field related to matter, while the electromagnetic quantum vacuum is related to all physical creation.

To understand such theories, the pattern of information that creates massless particles should be assessed. In particle physics, the two known massless particles are the photon (carrier of electromagnetism) and the gluon (carrier of the strong force). Both are types of known gauge bosons. Elementary particles interact with each other by the exchange of gauge bosons, usually as virtual particles. These virtual particles are created by the perturbation of a quantum field. Briefly, a perturbation occurs when a specific locale of a quantum field changes its frequency or excitation, thus creating a particle from "nothing." The "nothing" is, in fact, an oscillation of a quantum field locale, as described by the perturbation theory. (See Goswami 2011.)

In sacred geometry, it is understood that creation develops from geometrical structures, which can be holograms in the third dimension, albeit a fully formed object or entity in a much more subtle plane. The information contained in the waves of creation expresses itself into geometric shapes.

Apart from being created by holographic geometric shapes, particles are also either a particle or a wave. Drawing on the notion of particle-wave duality, it is suggested that upon eating food, the physical body will absorb the particle, while the etheric body will absorb the wave and, consequently, its information in the form of geometric holograms. Equally, the information that was passed through the animals' etheric bodies are casualties of the environment and of their own feelings, but the information that generated every atom of their meat will also be absorbed as information by whomever eats it.

In metaphysics, meat is created by astral factors intended to help the spirit express its potentials in matter. The first molecules to become flesh in a living body are designed to strengthen intention, impede obstacles, and guarantee courage. Literally, the reason "flesh"—that is, "muscle"—exists is to enable willpower to manifest in the physical plane. The muscles in animals, as well as in humans, have this physiological task: to guarantee the force of intention and action in matter. The greater someone's muscle mass is, without the need for physical exercise or dietary supplements, the greater is their strength of intention.

When the muscle is forcibly removed from the animal, that is, when the animal's force of intention is "used" by someone other than the owner of that muscle, that force (muscle) etherically becomes its antiversion by having its polarities changed. Flesh, therefore, turns into apathetic and pessimistic matter. The geometry that initially formed those elementary particles from a quantum state, as a result, spins all of its holograms in their opposite directions. Such movement is not creative, which means that the piece of meat will not physically metamorphose into a different physical element, although its etheric version will.

Reasonably, questions may arise with regard to carnivorous animals in nature. However, the etheric life cycle of those animal's molecules of meat and tissues ends at the moment an animal kills the other. This is determined by the habitat's morphogenetic programming system (see Sheldrake 2011). In addition, the muscles and organs of animals are used in accordance with their natural needs before and during their physical deaths, as opposed to adapting to the artificial arrangements developed by animal husbandry.

# 5     Animal Sacrifice

Animal sacrifice is the offering of an animal's life in a ritualistic ceremony. Sacrificial slaughter has been present in numerous religions across the world since ancient times, from the Hebrews, Greeks, Romans, Egyptians, Aztecs, and Yoruba, to various contemporary cults.

The rituals in which animals are sacrificed often endeavor to appease a specific entity, god, or even to thank nature and the divine for what has been given. The ultimate purpose of a sacrifice is to supply a supernatural being with elements, thereupon a particular desire can be granted.

According to Flores (1999) religious slaughter first appeared in the Badari culture of Egypt, which flourished between 4400 and 4000 BCE. According to German scholar Walter Burkert (1983), religious sacrifices may have derived from hunting practices, where hunters, feeling guilty for killing an animal, would try to mitigate their responsibility in these rituals, making their gods part of it and, therefore, be relieved of culpability. According to this theory, the hunters would also ease their consciences by suggesting that everybody should participate in the killing of the sacrificial victim. These justifying practices were especially identified in ancient Greece and Rome.

After the introduction of ritualistic animal slaughter, countless religions adopted the practice for the sole act of propitiation or worship, to incur divine favor or avoid divine retribution. Different doctrines promoting animal sacrifice affirm that their deities would normally require specific victims. For instance, it has been noted by Krause (1931) that the ancient Roman gods, with the exception of Mars, Neptune, Janus, and the Genius, were offered castrated male animals as offerings. Conversely, the female deities were presented with female offerings. Juno, the goddess of marriage and childbirth, was customarily presented with white cows or heifers. The choice of offerings for the gods was also symbolic, with white animals being offered to the gods above, the ones with dark hides being given to gods associated with the night, and red offerings being presented to Vulcan, the god of fire, and Robigo, the goddess of grain rust (Rüpke 2007).

In Western African cults, such as those seen in the Yoruba cultures and African diaspora religions, each deity would be offered their favorite animal (Johnson 2002). In Caribbean countries, namely Jamaica and Cuba, religions such as *obeah* and *palo,* respectively, make use of animal sacrifices such as roosters and rams. In palo, even the remains of humans, such as skulls and skin, are often found within the offerings (Santo et al. 2013). Other traditions in the Americas, such as Haitian Vodou, Louisiana Voodoo, and Brazilian Candomblé, are also known for sacrificing animals to pay homage to Orishas.

Animals would also be sacrificed in rituals not aimed to please a deity, but to heal a disease, where a priest and other entities would transfer the individual's disease to the animal, who after being killed would take the disease with it. Other ritualistic slaughter includes the promotion of prosperity and the breaking of malignant spells.

Though rare, in the eastern states of India, animal sacrifice is also offered to the goddess Durga during the Hindu festival of Navratri. It is believed that the sacrifice stimulates her violent vengeance against the buffalo demon (Fuller 2004, 46, 83–85). Nevertheless, these sacrifices are rare and most of them have usually been substituted by vegetarian offerings.

Although it is often assumed that ancient cultures may have offered animal sacrifices for nature to change its course, it is important to consider that, in those religions, every aspect of nature had one or multiple deities as their creators and rulers. For instance, in the old Aztec religion, Tlaloc is the god of rain; in the old Scandinavian religion, Njord is the god of the sea; and in Persian Zoroastrianism, Vayu-Vata are two gods often paired together; the former is the god of wind and the latter is the god of the atmosphere and air. Thus, a sacrificed offering aimed at changing the course of nature must be assumed as an offering to nature's governors.

In modern days, the term *witchcraft* has acquired different connotations, symbolizing both the classical malevolent conjurer or even individuals involved with the New Age movement. Nevertheless, witchcraft rituals associated with animal sacrifices commonly occur within black magic,* which can be identified in diverse cultures and periods of history, regardless of location or its devotees' racial backgrounds.

Black magic, or "low magic," is normally understood as the counterpart of white magic, or "high magic." The origins of black magic can be traced to the primitive worship of spirits in various populations (Place and Guiley 2009). Unlike white magic, which has traditionally been used for selfless purposes, black magic is used in order to receive selfish outcomes.

An important parallel between animal slaughter in black magic and in ancient and modern cults is that ritualistic sacrifices of animals (and humans) are invariably assisted by discarnate spirits of humans.

In a ritual where something is offered to an entity, the aura between the offerer and the entity is embedded in a phenomenon similar to what is known as quantum entanglement. Thus, the offerer's intention allows the offering to be assigned to that specific entity, preventing any third party from potentially seizing the offering for themselves.

During a ritualistic offering where there is no slaughter, chants, candles, incense, symbols, and hymns may be used so that the etheric double of the elements offered can be displaced, absorbed, or utilized by the offered entity. All matter has a holographic counterpart in the astral realm—that is, its exact copy is called its "etheric double" (Leadbeater 1902).

---

*"Black magic," in this case, refers to magic in the absence of light (also known as "dark magic"); thus, it does not relate to any African Diaspora cultures, ethnicities, or religions.

## THE SPIRITUAL USE OF ANIMAL ENERGY

Contrary to widely held belief, spirits given offerings neither eat nor drink the offerings. They normally manipulate the etheric double of the offered elements, whereby they energetically fabricate the worshipper's request into a sort of thought-form. In most cases, when placing a request, the worshipper generates a thought-form. Following this, the being addressed magnetizes that hologram with the manipulated energies that were obtained from the elements present in the offering. As the thought-form gains energy and magnetism, it spontaneously starts to attract future probabilities of what was initially requested (Barreto 2019).

It is crucial to emphasize that ordinary discarnate spirits *do not* have the ability to manipulate the elements of an offering, should any be given to them. Therefore, they need master the art of energy manipulation between the planes before being able to receive an offering. As for ordinary spirits—that is, spirits of discarnate individuals who do not play a role in religious or spiritualistic practices—the *only way* they can absorb energies from the physical plane is by the use of energy vampirism from a living person or animal. It is also important to understand that offerings made to a deity or divine being are only received by the spirits aligned with their sphere of influence. The authorization for the manipulation of offerings is conveyed telepathically, either directly by the deity or through a spirit of higher hierarchy, in instances where the specified god not exist.

When the offering consists of an animal's life, entities typically absorb the etheric body of the animal upon slaughter. The dead physical body is of no use to the entity, and the animal's astral body normally "leaves" the scene, escorted by benevolent rescuers or attracted to immediate reincarnation.

Often, the animals sacrificed in religious ceremonies are those who possess at least an astral body, which is the replica of the physical body (or its matrix). In between the animal's astral and physical bodies lies the etheric body. The etheric body functions as the intermediate layer of the astral and physical bodies, serving to animate the physical body with more subtle aspects of the spirit, as well as passing to the astral body all the repercussions of physical interaction and experiences. In the etheric body, the currents of qi (or chi, prana, or life force) travel by the virtue of canals and the chakras—the energy vortices.

The etheric body consists of several layers of what is known as vital energy; however, most of it is in the form of ectoplasm (Xavier 1945). Ectoplasm is a semiphysical gas, often characterized as a gelatinous, albeit extremely subtle fluid. All animals have ectoplasm, which is substantially produced by the physical body and, to some extent, by the astral body. This fluid is exceptionally powerful, as it serves to not only invigorate physical bodies but also has the power to potentiate the fabrication of objects in the astral realms. More importantly, it may give discarnate spirits, both the ordinary and the powerful malignant ones, the physical sensations experienced in the material world, as well as energy to reign, dominate, and protect themselves in the lower zones of reality.

Countless maladjusted and malignant spirits flock to slaughterhouses in search of ectoplasm and the remains of the etheric bodies of slaughtered animals. Not only does the unfortunate vibration of those who suffer there serve to fuel the wrath of some vengeful spirits, their energetic remains are a powerful tool for such wicked disincarnates.

The creation of mental images of animals about to die is mainly related to fear. These images are used by some spirits who, when introducing their vengeful and controlling spells into the physical world, exert profound influence on wars and epidemics. Similarly, other vampire spirits, who were possibly bloodthirsty psychopaths in their past lives, use the remaining etheric bodies of slaughtered animals to feed themselves and thus experience carnal sensations. Many other spirits extremely attached to the vices of doing evil also gather in the corridors of the slaughterhouses, rejoicing in the midst of the semiphysical energies of so numerous corpses.

During the ritualistic slaughter, the animal's etheric body is not conserved into the shape of a body, but as a mist that would otherwise be absorbed by the Earth's etheric fields if not promptly abducted by an entity. The spirits who demand animal slaughter as offerings are generally malignant spirits, since low magic stems from selfishness that disregards the lives and the pain of others—in this case, of sacrificed animals.

Fig. 5.1 a. In sacrifices with animal slaughter, entities normally abduct the remains of the victim's etheric body.

Fig. 5.1 b. In sacrifices without animal slaughter, entities manipulate the etheric double of the elements offered. Illustrations by David Barreto.

The word *sacrifice* may signify either a sacred slaughter or the sacred offering of anything, such as food, libations, or objects. In several healing practices involving animal sacrifice, there are magic rituals that allegedly pass one's illness to the energetic body of an animal, which once dead is presumed to take the disease with it. Admittedly, the afflicted individual will experience a relative improvement of their condition; however, the technique of "body-swapping" is constructed on a misinterpretation of what occurs in reality.

Initially, the ritual coalesces the external layers of the aura of both the human and the animal, where the maladies of the first are shared with the latter. Subsequently, the animal's etheric body, which is absorbed by the entity, serves to invigorate the spirit performing the ritual. From then on, this entity reserves a certain amount of ectoplasm to produce kinds of etheric adhesives and binders to be applied to the individual's own etheric body. However, as the illness is generated in the astral body, the amelioration of symptoms is temporary. Therefore, the result of "body exchange" is of limited efficacy.

As observed in numerous religions and cults, the practice of making offerings for gods, nature, and spirits is common. In certain faiths, the offering may include cuts of meat from an animal that was not ritualistically slaughtered.

The meats placed on an offering do not possess ectoplasm. However, as they are still physical elements, they do have a nonphysical counterpart. Therefore, the elements of the offering are used to mold thought-forms or create holograms of future probabilities.

The subtle counterpart of meat is dense in its constitution. This means that the meat's etheric elements will assuredly be used to produce dense objects. Among these diabolical objects are the elementars and even energetic strings that connect individuals in "love-binding" spells.

In cults where pieces of meat are used in spiritual cleansing rituals, it is believed that the dense energies of someone or somewhere would be directed to the flesh, as spiritual entities assist such maneuvering of energies. Although meat is not a highly recommended cleansing tool, since it etherically decomposes and pollutes, this kind of ritual is the closest to reality regarding what really occurs in the invisible realms. The utilized piece of meat is undoubtedly discarded after the ritual, and in its natural decaying process the malefic energies attached to it are understood to be transmuted and reabsorbed into the streams of ether.

The entities responsible for the cleansing will normally be prepared to handle the pernicious elements, to avoid morbidities caused by meat's own negative aura. Nevertheless, most sects that take part in this practice are not aware that, frequently, the entities behind requests for raw meat may have dubious intentions.

Religions that sacrifice animals may argue that the "energy" of the animal goes to the gods; however, this argument is strongly camouflaged by their exceedingly dogmatic rituals, sacrificial regalia, and archaic fundamentals.

Although individuals may feel distressed about these ritualistic activities, animal sacrifice for occult reasons varies little from slaughtering animals for food.

# 6 Animal Worship in Ancient Religions

Most ancient religions, especially those that thrived in ancient civilizations, were associated with animal adoration. In some cultures, animals were said to be symbols of the gods; in others, animals personified the gods themselves. Numerous animals became mystical models, as in lucky pets, while others were said to bring bad luck or foreboding. The general evidence is that when an ancient religion portrayed an animal in its rites or myths, the sole beneficiary invariably was humans. In this chapter, examples obtained from ancient Egyptian, Indian, and Chinese religions demystify allegories and attributes given to animals, supporting the understanding of the real reason they were used as a heavenly expression, despite never enjoying equal treatment to the humans who adored their symbolism or their alleged relationship with the divine.

## EGYPT: ICONOGRAPHY

In ancient Egypt, the vast majority of gods were portrayed as having the head of an animal and the body of a human being. This is amply observed on temple walls, ornaments, religious statues, and papyrus scriptures. A diversity of animals constituted the pantheon of the civilization on the banks of the Nile River.

In the dynastic period between 3100 BCE to 2686 BCE, Anubis—god of death, mummification, embalming, life after death, cemeteries, tombs and the underworld in general—was depicted in the form of a complete animal, with the head and body of a jackal. After that period, the god began to be portrayed only with the head of the animal, acquiring a humanoid body (Wilkinson 1999).

Predominantly, as Cline and Rubalcaba (2004) explain, the Egyptians of the middle and upper classes would have a pet dog, as they believed that the presence of the animal, related to Anubis, could not only repel death, but also guarantee a satisfying and luxurious afterlife. Nevertheless, stray dogs or someone else's dogs were typically ignored or just seen as mere animals.

Although the correlation between animals and gods, especially in ancient pantheons, was based upon the personalities of the animals and the gods—as if one reflected the aspects of the other—in ancient Egypt the subject had much more to do with a worldly view than properly with the divine.

In predynastic Egypt, when the dead were buried in shallow graves, the region's wild dogs would dig up the graves to eat the corpses. Thus, these animals were strongly associated with cemeteries. According to Wilkinson (1999) this explains the early correlation between Anubis and dogs and jackals.

Yet another example demystifying the erroneous idea that animals in ancient Egypt were considered sacred relates to Ra, who was believed to rule in all realms: heaven, earth and the underworld. The god was portrayed as having the body of a human and the head of a falcon.

According to mythology, Ra would illuminate the underworld for twelve hours each day. When he would reappear at dawn on the eastern horizon, he would take the form of a falcon (Haikal n.d.). Ra, the god of the kings, had a symbolic appearance based on his creations, the sky and the earth. Thus falcons, with their allegorical ability to fly as high as the midday sun, privileged with panoramic eyesight of Ra's creations, were the perfect fit for illustrating the god.

Nut, goddess of the sky, the stars, the cosmos, astronomy, and the universe, was represented by the image of a celestial cow. Contrary to what may be believed, Nut did not share characteristics with cows. Before countless misleading characteristics were attributed to her, Nut was just a deity known as the agent of great causes.

According to mythology, Ra was tired of having to rule ungrateful humanity; he thus asked Nut to take him to the highest heavens. Bewildered, Nut hesitated, as she did not know how to go about such a task. But the god Nun, father of Ra, obligated her, transforming the goddess into a celestial cow (Pinch 2004). The symbolism of a cow was correlated to that of a carrier, as cows would mostly serve as carriers and cart wagon pullers in ancient Egypt. Additionally, receiving the denomination of a celestial goddess was intrinsically associated with the task Nut had performed under the orders of Nun. Celestial cows therefore suggested the carrier to the highest heavens.

Nut was also depicted wearing a water pot as a headdress. The pot, which can be found in the hieroglyph of part of her name, may have symbolized the uterus (Redford 2001); however, the pot may also have represented the water carried by the cows, as well a bucket of milk. Being represented as a celestial cow, Nut was subsequently linked to maternity. Nevertheless, the only reason Nut was initially linked with the image of a cow was by virtue of being the carrier of Ra; maternal characteristics were later added to her qualities.

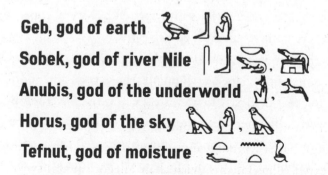

Fig. 6.1. Hieroglyphs of notorious Egyptian gods. Notice the parallel between the deities and the animals used to symbolize them. Illustration by David Barreto.

The goddess Bastet was originally portrayed as a lioness, an attribute she shared with Sekhmet. Eventually, Sekhmet came to represent the powerful warrior and protective aspect of a lioness. Bastet, who kept her cult following, was left with a more gentle and domesticated personality, and so started to be more related to domesticated cats.

Once represented as a cat, Bastet saw her personality adapted around the personality of cats. Thus, Bastet became the Egyptian goddess of the home, domesticity, and women's secrets. Fertility has also become one of Bastet's attributes, as cats can procreate several times in one lifetime.

Mafdet, another feline goddess, was one of the first Egyptian deities to be portrayed as a cat, and she was often depicted wearing the skin of a cheetah. She was venerated for protecting against the bite of snakes and scorpions. Later, those qualities would pass to Bastet.

One of the main reasons why worshippers venerated Bastet was for her role in keeping homes protected from evil spirits and disease. Again, Bastet is an example of the ordinary animal providing the divine with their mundane features. Before being revered as a domestic cat, Bastet had no connection with pests, diseases, or even home life, yet as domesticated cats keep pests away—especially mice and small snakes—these traits became some of the most renowned attributes of Bastet.

Ultimately, most of the gods of ancient Egypt who were portrayed as animals were, in fact, gods who poorly shared their divine characteristics with their representations on Earth. They were, thus, the victims of misinterpreted mythological correlations.

Nevertheless, it is crucial to highlight that regardless of being dressed, named, and shaped by humans, those gods and goddesses were, and still are, real deities. Their existence was not invented by humans, but discovered. Neither were their divine qualities compromised by a constantly modified appearance. It is also accepted that several gods and goddesses developed a different image and, consequently, new characteristics as a result of a better understanding by their cults. That may suggest the possibility that the god's altered qualities were more accurate as to their nature—as opposed to their primitive, initial descriptions.

## A Cryptic Fraud

Undeniably, the Egyptians venerated hawks and falcons, since these were the supreme portraits of Ra. However, while worshippers of Ra wondered whether wild hawks and falcons flying high were Ra himself, on the Earth those same animals were often treated cruelly.

The Egyptians would mass-breed raptors to give them as votive offerings to the gods. Not only were falcons, hawks, and kestrels kept in captivity for the sole purpose of being given as offerings, they were also force-fed to have a generous last meal before being mummified. The purpose of an excessive last meal was, assuredly, to appease the gods further. The birds would commonly choke to death. In contrast, other worshippers would prefer to have the animal gutted instead of force-feeding them a last meal, replacing their organs with other objects. It must be mentioned that the animals being gutted were not killed before undergoing such a process (Ikram et al. 2015; McKnight et al. 2015).

When beloved pet cats died, they were embalmed, coffined, and buried in cat cemeteries (Baldwin 1975). However, despite being regarded as the living incarnation of Bastet, some cats were raised in captivity in order to be offered to the gods. Votive cats were, like falcons and other birds, given to the very goddesses they represented. As offerings or as company for deceased pharaohs, they were mummified (fig. 6.2, p. 82), which also included the occasional force-feeding to death, or rarely gutting, having their organs substituted by jewelry (Ikram 2005). The widespread presence of cat mummies in ancient Egypt highlights the significance of the cat cult in the country's economy. This cult necessitated the breeding of cats and the establishment of a trading network for the provision of food, oils, and resins required for their mummification (Ikram 2015).

During the Hellenistic period between 323 and 30 BCE, the goddess Isis became associated with Bastet and cats. An inscription at the Temple of Edfu reads: "Isis is the soul of Bastet." In this period, Engels (1999, 33) says cats were systematically bred to be killed and to be mummified as sacrifices to the gods yet the Greek historian Diodorus Siculus (90–30 BCE) stated that killing a cat in Egypt was regarded as a serious crime. Between 60 and 56 BCE, Egyptians expressed their outrage by

Fig. 6.2. Mummified cat.
Photo by David Barreto.

lynching a Roman soldier who had killed a cat, despite the efforts of
Pharaoh Ptolemy XII Auletes to protect the man (Burton 1973).

During Egypt's first dynasty, circa 3218–3035 BCE, not only were
animals sacrificed as part of the funerary rituals of pharaohs, but also
humans. Both were thought to assist the pharaoh in a luxurious after-

life. Fee retainers have been found buried near each pharaoh's tomb as well as animals sacrificed for the burial. The tomb of Djer, pharaoh of the First Dynasty, is identified with the burials of 338 individuals.

A typical transgression among ancient cults in Egypt was the parallel created between honorable priests and misguided believers (including pharaohs), who ultimately perceived ritualistic customs based on religious claims that were specific to a particular context, as opposed to universal truths. In Egypt, numerous priests would support human or animal sacrifice, but their suggestions were often disregarded by many, including other priests.

Sacrifice in ancient Egypt was prohibited by 380 CE, after a series of decrees and edicts issued by Roman emperors in the fourth and fifth centuries CE (Tomorad 2015).

Concerning the diet of the ancient Egyptians, according to Balkwill (1994), the rich would have extravagant suppers replete with meat, while the poor would have vegetables and a much more moderate amount of meat. The lower class would also raise animals to be used exclusively for food. Among the most consumed meats in ancient Egypt were the meat of hippopotamus, gazelle, bull, duck, and fish. Many priests would abstain from consuming steak. Hippopotamuses and oxen/cows, who shared their images with, respectively, Taweret and Nut, were not spared for their appearance or similarities with the gods. Herds were fattened and slaughtered without ceremony or any liturgy.

The Egyptians did not worship animals as deities, but solely their images. Whether as sacrifices, food, or forced labor, the animals of ancient Egypt themselves were, without exception, not worshipped. Their connection with the gods was only their iconography, which served to facilitate people's understanding of the powers of each god.

## INDIA: SYNERGY

In the Hindu religion, both in ancient and present times, animals are recurring figures in the worship of the divine. Some animals give shape to the gods; others are considered as the reincarnation of people. Hinduism widely accepts the concept of metempsychosis, which is the theory that the spirit could regress to animal form as punishment.*

Hinduism is the oldest major religion in the world that remains active. As Hinduism has survived the millennia—unlike the religions of ancient Egypt and ancient China—the concepts that characterized its gods partially as animals date back to the beginning of Hinduism itself.

Several Hindu gods are portrayed as animals or have their characteristics: Ganesha has the head of an elephant; Lord Narasimha is half lion; Hayagriva has the head of a horse; Garuda has the head of a bird; Lord Varaha is a boar; Matsya is a fish; and Hanuman is a monkey (Harshananda 1987).

In Hinduism—like in ancient Egypt and Mesopotamia—when a god is portrayed as an animal, the allegorical correspondence serves to underscore the god's most salient qualities.

For example, it is observed that the god Ganesha's portrayal as an elephant encouraged his cult to spread over the millennia, when only a fraction of the population could read. The presence of allegorical images were crucial for followers to understand the qualities of the gods.

The legend of Ganesha is widely recognized in Hindu mythology and is documented in the Shiva Purana, translated by Shastri in 1950. The story begins with Parvati, the goddess, preparing for a bath. To ensure she would not be disturbed, she formed a boy from turmeric paste taken from her body and breathed life into him. The boy was then instructed to guard the door and prevent anyone from entering until Parvati had finished bathing.

When Shiva, Parvati's husband, returned from his meditation and tried to enter, he was stopped by the boy. Despite explaining his relationship to Parvati, the boy refused to let Shiva enter. Shiva, sensing

---

*The ideology may have arisen as an unconscious remembrance. Some believe that ancient humans had a spiritual exile to Earth. According to this idea, the hostile and disruptive spirits who were hindering the enlightenment of planets that were imminently advancing in terms of principles and love could no longer reincarnate on those orbs for lack of vibratory compatibility. Those spirits were temporarily compelled to incarnate on less advanced planets, such as Earth, so that they could self-discipline while helping this world advance its progress. Subsequently, some returned to their homelands and others migrated, but most have now left Earth (Xavier 1939a).

the boy was not ordinary, engaged in a fight with him and ultimately severed the boy's head with his trident.

Upon learning what had happened, Parvati was furious and threatened to destroy all of creation. Lord Brahma intervened and begged her to reconsider. Parvati agreed to do so on the conditions that the boy be brought back to life and forever worshipped before all other gods. In accordance with her wishes, Shiva ordered his Shiva-dutas to bring back the head of the first creature they found lying with its head facing north to replace the boy's lost head. The Shiva-dutas returned with the head of a powerful elephant, which Lord Brahma placed onto the boy's body, giving him new life. The boy was then named Gajanana and granted the status of being foremost among the gods and leader of all classes of beings.

Ganesha is remover of obstacles, patron of the arts, sciences, and learning, and god of beginnings. The mouse is usually Ganesha's "vehicle animal," which refers to wisdom, talent and intelligence. It also symbolizes the detailed investigation of enigmatic subjects, as mice lead secret lives below ground. The mouse serves to show how wisdom is needed to overcome the erratic mind.

Ganesha portrays a generous figure. He is described as holding round sweets, which he is excessively fond of, and which represent prosperity. His trunk suggests flexibility and his large ears exemplify omniscience (Harshananda 1987). Based on the portraits of Ganesha, it is noticed that his image is a theatrical illustration of his divine aspects.

Decoding Hindu gods is a complicated task, as their portraits typically exhibit many details and figurative messages in just one image.

The elephant is an animal of excellent memory and intelligence—thus, the god received the head of such animal. It was also believed that mice frightened elephants—hence, Ganesha had a mouse as his vehicle, which signifies that Ganesha is courageous enough to defeat such dread. Despite elephants being considered the incarnation of the Lord Ganesha, the animals often serve as symbolism for devout humans or as profitable assets for a few who exploit them for religious spectacles. (See the film *Gods in Shackles,* directed by Iyer and Cook 2016; see also Nidhin 2016.)

Hindus also believe in ten avatars of Lord Vishnu. One of these avatars of Vishnu is Rama, who was created to destroy Ravana, the ruling demon of Lanka (Lochtefeld 2001, 224, 265, 520). To help Rama, Lord Brahma ordered some gods and goddesses to take the form of monkeys. Thus Indra, Surya, Vrihaspati, and Pavana were reincarnated as the monkeys Bali, Sugriva, Tara, and Hanuman respectively.

The half-human, half-animal is a synergy noticeably present in Hinduism and in mythical figures from ancient Egypt, Greece, and numerous other cultures.

The image attributed to Hanuman is a mixture of the rhesus and the langur primates with human features. Hanuman has the most impressive and attractive aspects of each: the highly arched tail of the langur and the pink face with the most pronounced muzzle of the rhesus, as well as the posture of a human being. The god of courage, Hanuman has the physical characteristics of agile and athletic-looking monkeys (Greene 2013). Appearing as an extremely skilled being provided the god with the quickness to fight and to engage in battles, which were likely to be won triumphantly by the energetic avatar. Characteristics of just one species were inadequate to portray a character as brave as Hanuman's. Combining a human with an animal, whose qualities give believers an improved understanding of a deity's personality, was thus needed to advance the cult of gods. The qualities of three species were used to represent Hanuman's appearance. Nevertheless, the god emerged simple and primitive. This suggests that illustrators and sculptors played a significant role in developing Hindu gods, and, perhaps, some of the many characteristics of each god may have merely been supposed after their portraits were made.

### An Industrial Paradox

In Hinduism, animal sacrifice to the gods used to be commonplace, until the Buddha appeared and began to spread ideas of nonviolence and the idea that animal sacrifice contradicted divine love. Nevertheless, it is important to note that animals are still killed for nonreligious purposes in India and within Hindu communities

(Ministry of Fisheries, Animal Husbandry and Dairying [of India] 2020).

Cows are worshipped as a result of the historical need of Indians to maintain a continuous source of food and labor. A cow that was killed meant that a valued agricultural laborer and source of milk would cease; thus, the idolatry of cows began (contrary to the idea that cow idolatry had started as a religious factor). A religious meaning was later merged with the necessity of having what the cow could provide. It is still observed in modern days that cows will normally not be killed in India; however, they may still be seen pulling wagons, carrying loads, and more notoriously, producing milk (Ministry of Fisheries, Animal Husbandry and Dairying [of India] 2020).

Kamadhenu is considered the mother of all cows and a major symbol of prosperity. She is a miraculous cow of plenty who provides whatever her owners desire. All cows are venerated in Hinduism as the earthly embodiment of the Kamadhenu. As such, Kamadhenu is not worshipped independently as a goddess, and temples are not dedicated to her honor alone; rather, she is honored by the veneration of cows in general throughout the observant Hindu population. Kamadhenu was therefore introduced to the scriptures for the need to symbolize cows as holy, as well as the embodiment of prosperity.

Although goats also provide labor and milk, cows produce considerably higher amounts of milk—for this reason, goats were seen as a source of meat instead.

The festival of Kali Puja in eastern India holds a special significance for the Hindu deity Kali. In parts of Bengal, Orissa, and Assam, the tradition of animal sacrifice continues to be performed during the festival. Within temple precincts, animals are mercilessly sacrificed (Fuller 2004, 83).

Despite being the vehicle of Goddess Kali, goats are sacrificially offered, exhibiting yet again the recurring paradox of cults that symbolize the divine with animals while slaughtering them. It is important to emphasize that the practice is dramatically becoming less common throughout India. Many types of meat are used in Indian cuisine. Chicken, fish, and mutton tend to be the most commonly consumed meats. Buffalo meat consumption is prevalent in some parts of the country, such as coastal areas as well as the northeast. (See the report by T&A Consulting 2017.) The noneating of cow's meat, however, is what makes most people conceptualize India as a predominantly vegetarian nation.

Anthropological surveys conducted in 2018 by Balmurli and Suraj estimate that only twenty percent of Indians are vegetarians. Due to cultural and political pressures, citizens report eating less meat, especially beef, while they report eating more vegetarian food.

Hindus are known to worship cows as goddesses since they correlate these animals with motherhood, kindness, and tolerance. Therefore, killing a cow is strictly prohibited in Hinduism. Cow's milk is also considered pure and is hence is used to bathe the deities' images. According to Foster (1889) even cow urine and excrement are also considered to be pure and are adopted in various rituals. Additionally, the god Shiva is also called by another name, *Gorakhnath,* which means God of Cows.

By contrast, buffaloes, close relatives of cows, are related to Yama, the Lord of Death—hence people do not invite them into their homes, as they do to cows. Hindus, therefore, do eat buffalo meat and drink their milk. The reason for such apparent ambiguity may be due to the late introduction of wild buffaloes in the Indian culture, which occurred millennia after cows were part of the Hindu domesticated herd.

Although India may be stereotyped for the people's esteem for cows, it should be noted that the country is the largest producer and consumer of dairy in the world—both of buffaloes and cows, accounting for 18.5% of the world's production (Laveesh 2009, 30). The production of dairy in India by species, according to M. F. Fuller (2004, 589), is as follows: indigenous buffalo (35%), cross-bred cows (26%), nondescript buffalo (14%), nondescript cows (10%), indigenous cows (10%), goat (4%), exotic cows (1%). India is also one of the largest beef exporters in the world, exporting mostly buffalo meat.

According to the 2014 Indian census, more than 80% of Indians declare themselves to be Hindus; however, the allegories present in Hinduism with regard to the treatment of animals do not always affect the eating habits of the nation. According to the 2014 national census, 71% of Indians who describe themselves as Hindus are not vegetarian. According to official national research, vegetarianism is mostly observed among the higher classes (according to the Department of Animal Husbandry & Dairying's 2019 report).

It is important to stress that the general population cannot be blamed for such a disparity between those who eat meat and those who abstain. However, it is relevant to emphasize that farmed animals are not treated with as much appreciation as is shown in paintings and mythology in general, and this includes cows and the local dairy industry.

## Jainism

Jain dharma is one of the world's oldest continuously practiced religions. Founded in the sixth century BCE, Jainism is one of the oldest religions in India, along with Hinduism and Buddhism, sharing with the latter the absence of a god as a creator or central figure.

According to Jainism, the existence of "a bound and ever-changing soul" is a self-evident truth; an axiom that does not need to be proven. It maintains that there are numerous types of souls, but every one of them has three qualities: consciousness (the most important), bliss, and vibrational energy. It further claims that "vibrations" draw karmic particles to the soul, thus creating bondage, but this also adds merit or demerit to the soul. Jain texts also state that souls exist as "clothed with material bodies," and entirely fill up the body.

In Jainism as in other Indian religions, karma connotes the universal cause and effect law.

One of the main religious premises of the Jain dharma is "nonviolence," so as not to attract karma. The principle of nonviolence must be observed by Jains in thought, word, and deed on an individual and social level. Jains recognize that people, animals, plants, rock formations, water streams, and waterfalls have *jiva,* or soul, or a vital principle. All these beings have equal value and are interconnected in the web of existence by karmic links. Such principles lead its followers to a vegetarian lifestyle and to caring for and rescuing injured and abandoned animals.

Based on the categorizations of sentient beings and their perception of pain, the adepts of Jainism customarily will not even eat foods that may have harmed small insects on their way from the crops to the kitchen—for instance, in the case that the harvester stepped on a bug.

## DYNASTIC CHINA

In ancient China, the Shang dynasty ruled in the North China Plain, in the northeast of the country. It is believed that the Shang, the second dynasty, ruled approximately 13.5 million people during their reign (Hao 2011). According to Chinese tradition, this dynasty began in 1556 BCE and ended in 1046 BCE. (See Keightley's chapter in the 1999 book edited by Loewe and Shaughnessy on the Shang Dynasty.) The Shang were already powerful before succeeding the Xia dynasty (2070–1600 BCE). They were followed by the Zhou dynasty (1046–256 BCE). (See Loewe and Shaughnessy's chapter "Calendar and Chronology" in the 2008 book edited by Keightley.)

The Shang dynasty is the earliest dynasty of traditional Chinese history adamantly supported by archaeological evidence. Excavation at the ruins of Yin (identified as the last Shang capital and near modern-day Anyang) uncovered eleven major royal tombs, which included remains from both animal and human sacrifices. Thus, much of the information available about the Shang society has come to the surface as the findings of inscriptions made on bovine shoulder blades, or less commonly, on turtle shells. Oracles also recorded inscriptions on bones, which they used for divination. In the Xiaotun region, over 200,000 fragments of oracular bones have been uncovered, providing rich insight into the intricacies of the Shang state (Keightley 1990).

Chang (1976) explains that the burial practices of the Shang dynasty emperors involved interment in large cruciform tombs, necessitating the mobilization of significant human resources. The deceased were enclosed within wooden coffins and surrounded by a range of funerary objects. Archeological excavations of these tombs have uncovered the remains of human individuals, as well as those of dogs and horses, along the ramp leading to the tomb's interior. Yuan and Flad (2005) say that in that period, it was customary to sacrifice these animals in religious rituals to Shang Di (God).

In his 1989 book, Keightley says that the Shang people worshipped a considerable number of gods, many of whom were living royalty. Others were spirits of nature, some of whom were possibly derived from popular myths and local cults.

Only with the Zhou dynasty would the idea of a main god arise. The evidence discovered in the tombs clearly shows that the Shang believed in life after death and that oracular requests may have been directed to deceased ancestors (Loewe and Shaughnessy 1999, 232–91).

Keightley (1989) also says that the Shang court may have been frequented by shamans and it is possible that the emperor himself was a shaman. Should these views be legitimate, the essence of the Shang religion was assuredly different from the rational approach of the philosophical schools that would have become predominant during the Zhou period.

Chinese historians of later periods have become accustomed to the notion that one dynasty succeeded the other. However, it is known that the political situation in primitive China was much more complex. Numerous scholars suggest that the Xia and the Shang were perhaps political entities that coexisted, as the Zhou were contemporaries of the Shang (Loewe and Shaughnessy 1999). Both dynasties had animal sacrifices as a norm in their religious rituals.

According to Keightley (1989), the origin of the use of dogs as votive offerings developed from a primitive cult in honor of a dog-shaped vegetation god, whose worship later merged with that of Shang Di, the reigning divinity of the Shang pantheon—hence the systematic sacrifice of dogs at that time.

The excavations of Shang tombs around Anyang in 1928 revealed a large number of animal and human sacrifices. There was hardly one tomb or a consecrated building without the sacrifice of a dog. In Xiaotun, the bones of a total of 825 human victims, 15 horses, 10 oxen, 18 sheep and 35 dogs were unearthed (Yuan and Flad 2005). Dogs were usually buried wrapped in rushes and in lacquer coffins. The fact that sacrifices were mostly of dogs and domestic horses demonstrates the importance of these two animals to ancient Chinese society in religious terms. This is reflected in an expression still used in modern times, to "work like a dog" or "work like a horse." Often, the dogs were just puppies. Generally, the dogs were buried alive, as they would serve as the eternal guardian for that human in the afterlife (Yuan and Flad 2005). In a discovery in the ancient city of Zhengzhou, archaeologists found eight ditches containing the remains of 92 strung dogs, who were apparently buried alive (Best 2019). Only in the Han dynasty (206 BCE–220 CE) did clay dog figures replace the burial sacrifices.

Pigs, sheep, and goats were also sacrificed. However, this practice was only incorporated once sheep were introduced into China, shortly after the region began to establish trade routes with Indo-European regions, according to Liu and Chen (2012). Without special status or the right to live, it is an incontestable truth that sacrificed animals were not part of the religion, but mere votive elements, comparable to bowls of water and incense.

Inscriptions on Shang oracle bones concern the whereabouts of lost dogs. They also refer to the Ning rite during which a dog was dismembered to placate the four winds or honor the four directions, a sacrifice carried over into Zhou times and mentioned in the *Erya* (ancient Chinese dictionary).

The ancient Chinese also sacrificed dogs in rituals invented without the slightest doctrinal connection, as in the example of the *Nan* sacrifice to repel the plague: a dog was dismembered and its remains buried in front of the main gates of the capital. *Ba*'s sacrifice, to intercept evil, demanded that the emperor crush a dog under the wheels of his chariot. Certain rituals occasionally included the blood of dogs, which was used to swear pacts among nobles.

## Chinese Zodiac

One of the most prominent representations of animals in ancient China comes from the zodiac. The Chinese zodiac, which is a classification scheme based on the lunar calendar, assigns an animal and its qualities each year in a repeated twelve-year cycle. The twelve-year cycle is an approximation of Jupiter's 11.85-year orbital period (Loewe and Shaughnessy 1999).

The animals of the zodiac are the rat, ox, tiger, rabbit, dragon, snake, horse, sheep, monkey, rooster, dog, and pig. The order of the animals is explained with a folktale about how animals were summoned to heaven by Emperor Jade, who ruled the skies over China. Legend has it that Emperor Jade ran a race and required all animals to participate. The top twelve could, hence, own a place on the calendar. Although the rat was small, it won first place, after being carried on the ox's back. The pig took the last place, since it stopped on the way to eat. (See Eng 2019.)

The twelve animals are divided into six pairs. In each pair, the two animals are complementary and cannot be separated based on their balancing attributes and characteristics. While the rat is a symbol of wisdom, the ox is a symbol of diligence. While the tiger is a symbol of bravery and vigor, the rabbit symbolizes prudence. While the dragon is a symbol of strength and inflexibility, the snake symbolizes malleability and dexterity. While the horse is a symbol of persistence and indomitable will, the sheep is a symbol of peace and tranquility. While the monkey is a symbol of versatility, the rooster is a symbol of constancy. While the dog is a symbol of honesty, the pig symbolizes humor and wealth (Denisenko and Zheng 2021). The range of animals depicted reflects the characters that can be compared to people or resemble traits of the human personality—from the adored dragon, mythical animal and traditional Chinese mascot, to the lamentably abhorred rat; or from the dreadful snake to the harmless rabbit; or from the pig, eaten throughout the history of China, to the domesticated dog.

Since the Han dynasty, the zodiac animals have served as a mere correlation tool. With the exception of the legendary dragon, practically all the animals depicted were slaughtered for food, which demonstrates that, despite being celebrated each year, those animals were just symbols to facilitate the correlation of personality traits, being granted no special status.

In many parts of ancient China, says Katz (2008, 56) the killing of cattle and the consumption of cows was prohibited, as they were valued for their role in agriculture, similarly to what occurred in India. In modern days, this custom is still followed by a modest number of Chinese families. The eating of dog meat in China dates back around 500 years ago and possibly even earlier. (See the BBC's 2016 article for this timeline and also to read about a dog meat festival.) Additionally, in classical Chinese literature, dogs are generally described as treacherous, and they were used as an offering to the gods, as guards to those who died, and as food for the people. Chang (1977) says that in Ancient China, pigs, chickens, and bulls were the animals most commonly consumed by the people.

In a press release, Ahlfort (2011) writes that a team of geneticists of the Royal Institute of Technology in Stockholm, in a report written with geneticists of the Kunming Institute of Zoology in China, proposed that wolves were domesticated by humans in a region south of the Yangtze River. The findings run counter to theories placing the domestication of the canine in the Middle East (ScienceDaily 2011). However, it is suggested by Wayne and von Holdt (2012) that the domestication of wolves in China was for food purposes, as opposed to companions and agricultural laborer purposes in the Middle East, where archaeological findings date back to 14,000 BCE.

## Confucianism

Confucianism is one of China's greatest philosophical-religious, moral, and political traditions. Developed over two millennia, it has also had an enormous influence in Japan, Korea, and Vietnam.

A ritual system and social doctrine that aimed to remedy China's spiritual decay, Confucianism was created at a time of profound cor-

ruption and serious political upheaval. The notable importance attributed to Confucius in classical Chinese texts led the first Europeans
who arrived in the region to think that Confucius was in fact its
founder. However, such practices existed before Confucius. According
to Chinese tradition, Confucius represents the greatest exponent of that
philosophy and was, therefore, worthy of accreditation. (Read de Bary
and Bloom 1999 for more information.)

Confucianism emphasizes family ties and social harmony, rather
than a soteriology that projects man's hopes for a transcendent future.
According to Western scholars, Confucianism is a philosophical system
that regards "the secular as sacred" (Fingarette 1972). Life and rela-
tionships are seen as manifestations of the sacred and an expression of
morality. Thus, humanity has a transcendent anchor in the concept of
Tiān (天), which means sky or heaven, representing the order of the
universe.

Confucian liturgy regarding the worship of gods in public temples
is ancient. After confronting competing schools of thought during
the Warring States Period (475–221 BCE) and violent fighting under
Emperor Qin Shi Huangdi, Confucianism was decreed the "state philosophy" under Emperor Han Wudi (156–87 BCE), although it did not
prevent the progress of other religions in the empire until the founding
of the Republic of China in 1912 (Chen 2012).

Fan (2010) explains that concerning animals, it must be recognized
that Confucius, the reluctant founding figure who has always been
considered the "sage among the sages," left much to be desired on the
subject. For him, animals were not part of humans and, therefore, did
not deserve any philosophical mention. In the Confucian tradition, god
(Tiān; meaning "force above"), the heavens, and the spirits should have
all the attention and reverence, which plainly excluded animals. More
than being ignored, they were sacrificed in offerings to those on the list
to be venerated—God, the heavens, and the spirits.

Giving philosophic allowance to animals, or treating them dearly
in Confucian regions, explains Blakeley (2003), was seen as prioritizing them instead of prioritizing the heavens and, especially, the family.

According to that philosophy, if humans should live a life of spiritual development, the emotional mingling with animals should not occur, as an evolving human must expand this grace of evolution with the family and then with the rest of other humans.

Confucianism by no means proscribed the mistreatment of animals. On the contrary, it indicated benevolence and harmony toward all. Nevertheless, sacrifices were part of the Confucian way of life. Moreover, passages showing consideration to animals in the sayings of Confucius or Mencius, who has often been described as the "second sage," were almost nonexistent, except to mention animal sacrifice, ownership of animals as financial resources or laborers, and consumption of dog meat (Adler 1999).

Unlike Confucianism, which had ambiguous attitudes toward all forms of life, other Eastern belief systems demonstrated a lofty regard for animals. Present-day Chinese civilization may not provide the most beneficent environment for animals, but its distant history appears to have been far more progressive.

## Taoism

Taoism is a philosophical religion of Chinese origin that emphasizes living in harmony with *Tao* ("the Way").

Taoism, or Daoism, a term of Western coinage, designates the philosophical and mystical doctrines exhibited mainly in the works attributed to Laozi and Zhuangzi, composed between the fourth and third centuries BCE. The Taoist religion was institutionalized as such around the first century CE.

Taoism, which originated in China, is centered on the role and place of human beings, all creatures, and all phenomena in the universe. Over time, various interpretations and schools of the religion have emerged. Despite its widespread presence in China and its rich textual tradition, Taoism is relatively unknown compared to other major world religions.

In contrast to Confucianism, which places a strong emphasis on social order and strict rituals, Taoism focuses on achieving "perfection" through aligning with the natural, unplanned rhythms of the universe, referred to as "the Way" or "Tao" (also spelled Dao). The ethics of Taoism can vary among different schools, but generally emphasize spontaneity and the Three Treasures: compassion, simplicity, and humility. (Readers interested in Taoism should read Wang 2004.)

Anderson and Raphals (2007) write that, prior to the founding of the Taoist religion, pigs or ducks were sometimes offered as sacrifice to the spirits of the dead or to the gods. Those who had better financial conditions, that is, more animals, continued with the sacrifices. In traditional Chinese communities, animal sacrifices are still proceeding. Archaeologists have traced this practice back to distant antiquity. Among the animals mentioned are dogs, chickens, turtles, oxen, and sheep. There is little textual evidence that Taoists protested these practices.

It was the Taoist celestial master Zhang Daoling (34–156 CE) who rejected the idea of animal sacrifices to the gods. Today's offerings, therefore, are based on fruit, incense, and joss paper (ghost money), which is burned. In Taoism, some sects linked to local religions used to practice offering slaughter even though the tradition emphatically preached the nonkilling of animals. The sects that still use animals such as pigs, fish, and oxen as offerings are typically related to regional practices and folklore, diverging from true Taoism (Watson 2011).

## BUDDHISM

Buddhism encompasses a variety of traditions, beliefs, and spiritual practices largely based on the original teachings and philosophies attributed to the Buddha (563–482 BCE). The philosophy originated in ancient India between the sixth and fourth centuries BCE, then spread across Asia.

Based on the Indian principle of *ahimsa* (nonharming), the Buddha's ethics strongly condemn harming any sentient beings, including all animals. He thus condemned the animal sacrifice of the

Brahmins as well as hunting and killing animals for food (Harvey 2000, 157).

Although early Buddhist texts depict the Buddha as allowing monastics to eat meat, this was a result of monks begging for their food and thus accepting whatever food was offered to them. This meat, however, had to be "three times clean," which meant that "they had not seen, had not heard and had no reason to suspect that the animal had been killed so that the meat could be given to them" (Phelps 2004, 76). Indeed, this rule was not a promotion of a specific diet, but a rule against the actual killing of animals. Phelps (2004) further elaborates on a well-known division within the Buddhism of early times, arising from the actions of Devadatta, a Buddhist monk who was also the cousin and brother-in-law of the Buddha. Devadatta aimed to make vegetarianism mandatory; however, the Buddha held a different view: that vegetarianism should be promoted purely out of pure compassion toward animals. Furthermore, Buddha considered that gaining one's livelihood from the meat trade was unethical.

In the regions of Buddhist China, animals enjoyed freedom and the right to live, since the basis of Buddhism was the nonaggression to living beings, which prohibited the killing of animals, both for food and for rituals. The Buddha promulgated many teachings encouraging nonaggression to animals, especially with regard to diet and offerings. (The Buddha's phrases and teachings can be appreciated in Phelps 2004.) The Buddha's doctrine of nonaggression to animals was so tenacious that even the practice of sacrifices in Hindu India also stopped after his appeals. In modern times, Buddhists are usually vegetarians, abstaining from any food that causes animal suffering.

The Buddha is one of the most important religious references in terms of respect for animals. His teachings are still practiced; hence, Buddhist temples and restaurants do not offer or collect food that is not vegetarian.

# SHINTO

Shinto, or Shintoism, is a religion that originated in Japan.* In contemporary Japan, a significant portion of the population adheres to elements of Shintoism, which is viewed by many as a way of life rather than a formal religion (Breen and Teeuwen 2010). As a polytheistic doctrine, it revolves around the *kami*: "gods" or "spirits" believed to inhabit all things. Shinto preaches peace and purity, and, consequently, nonviolence against living beings.

In Shinto, many animals were used as a symbol of communication with the kami. The link between the kami and the natural world has led to Shinto being considered an animistic and pantheistic doctrine. Offner (1979) says that many kami are believed to have messengers, known as *kami no tsukai* or *tsuka washime,* and these are generally depicted as taking animal form.

Shinto tends to have a compassionate approach toward animals. Thus, animal sacrifices are not considered appropriate, as the shedding of blood is seen as a polluting act that necessitates purification (Nelson 1996, 64). This notion of purity is present in many facets of Japanese culture. Among the things regarded as particular pollutants in Shinto are death, the flaying alive of an animal, bestiality, and excrement (Nelson 1996, 206; Offner 1979, 104).

Various words, termed *imi-kotoba,* are also regarded as taboo, and people avoid speaking them when at a shrine; according to Bocking (1997) these include the word *shishi* ("meat").

In Shinto, respect for life, including the life of animals, is one of the foundations of belief; hence, medieval Japan was practically vegetarian. The Buddhist vegetarian philosophy eventually spread to the peasants. Those who were involved in the trade of slaughtering animals for food or leather faced discrimination.

National Japanese religions, such as Buddhism and Shinto, heavily

---

*Shintoism is not of Chinese origin, but of Japanese origin. It is often incorrectly perceived as a philosophy and doctrine of China.

promoted plant-based eating. Shinto also considers that eating the meat of animals is impure. But the rule extends only to the meat of land mammals, not marine animals (Lee, Choi, and Sun 2020).

## Summary of Customs Regarding Animals in World Religions

Ultimately, **Confucianism** emphasized human flourishing, while categorically ignoring the importance of animals, unless material affairs were to be discussed.

**Taoism** saw animals as emotional beings with souls. Worthy of human compassion, animals of numerous species experienced a certain degree of respect.

**Buddhism** introduced the importance of treating animals with thorough benevolence. Inspiring peaceful acts toward all creatures, the Buddha's philosophy promoted vegetarianism and other practices that aimed to deliver animals from cruel labor.

In Japan, **Shintoism** tends to consider animal mistreatment as an unclean act, seeing animal suffering as impure to the soul.

**India** and **Egypt** both cultivated polytheistic religions.

In the culture of **ancient Egypt,** gods were given the attributes of animals and animal sacrifice was common.

The **Hindu** people of India also assign animal attributes to their deities. Although species of animals, such as cows, are revered, many Indians still raise and consume animals as a source of food.

# 7  Animals in Mysticism

## TOTEMS

A *totem* is a spiritual being, sacred object, or symbol that serves as an emblem of a group, such as a family, a clan, or the lineage or the entire shamanic tribe. The term is derived from the Algonquian word *odoodem,* as is *dodem* in its Ojibwan derivation, meaning "his kinship group" (Merrill and Goddard 2002). A totem is generally understood as an animal spirit that an individual invokes, either for themselves or for the tribe. The invocation asks for, besides the spiritual presence of the animal in question, their special instincts and survival skills.

Indigenous tribes are composed of smaller groups that are united by descent and formed around a founding or ancestral member. This ancestor was sometimes a symbolic animal spirit that became the clan's totem. Other times the animal represented in the totem was not an ancestor (Goldenweiser 1910).

Clan totems, typically represented by local fauna and flora, hold a distinct affiliation with the tribe and its rich history. The inherent supernatural abilities of these totems serve as a navigational force, directing each clan to fulfill their individual duties and obligations within the tribe, as per the specific attributes of the represented animal (Goldenweiser 1910).

Misleading mystical schools attribute Western conceptualized archetypes to that of totems, assuming that a turtle symbolizes something slow, or that the rabbit connotes multiplication, or that the wolf is a hunter. Totems, however, differ from Asian or Eurocentric beliefs in their symbolism. As an example of how Native American tribes may perceive a totem, a clan accompanied by the turtle may endeavor to acquire the qualities of guardians of wisdom, legends, and mysteries within their ceremonies and practices. Thus, the true context is not that of the sluggard.

Unlike more complex Jungian archetypes, totems are seen by the summoner or the group as positive and beneficial symbols, discarding any negative attributes that the animal may present in its personality or nature. It is not paradoxical that a clan would invoke the totem of a rabbit for battle: even though the rabbit is presumed to be easy prey (archetype), the totem centralizes its meaning on the animal's cleverness and agility.

Totems may also be symbols that one needs during a specific period of life. Generally, these symbols are created by spirit guides, meaning that, in most cases, what is perceived is not the spirit of an animal but an image that aims to deliver a message, as the tribe is used to the idea of interpreting personality traits of the surrounding animals. The same method of delivering a message would not occur, for example, in a Spiritist ceremony, as the mediums are not familiar with animal symbolism but are acquainted with communication with spirits.

Upon summoning a totem, the individual or clan is bound to the morphogenetic fields of that species. (See my 2019 book, *The Supernatural Science* and Sheldrake's 2011 book, *The Presence of the Past* for more.) This enables them to absorb the mixture of thought-forms created by such animals, allowing them to act in accordance with the instincts of that species. Totems were originally part of the culture of the native peoples of North America, but the concept of invoking the presence of an animal for protection has since grown in esoteric and neopagan circles around the world.

Much more than a mere allusion to the essence of Native American culture, spirits of animals and even disembodied spirits of people who have morphed into the image of animals may hear the call of those who invoke them.

## The Shape-Shifting Phenomena
## in the Astral Planes

Thousands of sinister humanoid spirits experience a sort of metamorphosis upon finding themselves in the spiritual planes. Often, they involuntarily or voluntarily have their astral bodies shaped into the form of animals, which may feature traits such as a beak, horns, wings, and paws. The metamorphosis occurs according to the perception each spirit has of itself. In the astral realms, the change of appearance is readily executed by thoughts and how the individual feels they are. As condensed matter is not required to give shape to an astral body, thought waves effortlessly fabricate what is believed. (My 2019 book *The Supernatural Science* explores this in more depth.)

In this context, "astral-morphism" is a temporary change of one's spiritual appearance and not an evolutionary retrogression or conversion from a humanoid spirit to an animal spirit. Here is an example of why astral-morphism occurs: malicious and selfish politicians steal millions when incarnated, leaving many in poverty. Upon dying, their spirit may re-evaluate what was done with remorse. In this condition, the former politicians might develop a self-image of a vulture or rat, as guilt and the desire for self-punishment leads them to evaluate themselves as comparable to these animals. In most cases, the individuals remain as humanoid spirits, albeit featuring animal peculiarities.

At the lower zones of the Earth's astral dimension, destructive spirits deliberately morph into the appearance of monsters or ferocious animals, hence they can reign among suffering spirits and be respected through fear. Thus, the intention of invoking animal spirits who are protectors may also result in the presence of a metamorphosed spirit, instead of that of a real animal. Energetic vampirism is regularly the reason these consciousnesses disguise themselves in such ways.

Additionally, individuals with a certain psychic ability, although bearers of corrupting egos, may have visions of animal guardians, not realizing that these may be cases of humanoid-to-humanoid vampirism and not real guardian animal spirit.

Fig. 7.1. Demon Andras, illustrated in the book *Infernal Dictionary* by
J. Collin de Plancy, 1863. Many demons from Goetia are depicted as
being an astral-morphism (temporary blend) of animal and human forms.
The similarity of these illustrations with real extraphysical entities is remarkable.

## ELEMENTALS

The elementals of nature are etheric and astral beings who dwell in certain layers of the etheric and astral planes. Normally, elementals have aspects that resemble those of animals in nature. Elementals can either incarnate as primitive animals or, more typically, advance to higher levels on other planes of existence. Despite this, it is possible for some elementals to spontaneously vanish if their formation was designed to maintain or shape a portion of the terrestrial ecosystem. Despite the possibility that some discarnate animals may find themselves among elementals, typically this only occurs when such an animal is on the verge of migrating to a more advanced species; the time spent in such transitional zones allows them to acquire traces of the species they will incarnate as.

The primary function of the elementals is to maintain the balance between the subtle elements of the planet and support the transition of energies between the etheric dimensions and the physical dimension of the Earth. In addition to supporting the transit of etheric fluids, elementals are also progressing in their own evolutionary stages. They are experiencing in the elements of nature the modality of physical life, albeit still at an etheric level.

Some of these etheric animals are called salamanders,* sylphs, gnomes, and undines, representing the elements fire, air, earth, and water, respectively. However, many other animals comprise this vast group, which is

Fig. 7.2. Painting of a salamander unharmed in the fire, 1350.

*Legends connecting salamanders and fire likely originate from the tendency of salamanders to dwell inside rotting logs. When the log was placed into a fire, the salamander would attempt to escape, which led some to think that salamanders were created from flames (Ashcroft 2002, 112). Not all fiery elementals are referred to as salamanders, and most of them do not resemble salamanders or lizards of the physical third dimension.

commonly found in unspoiled nature, such as beaches and seas, forests and woods, mountains and valleys, fields and deserts. Many live in intra-terrestrial realities or magmatic chambers on the planet.

Elementals can be seen by humans via clairvoyance, and the etheric fluids that sustain their life-forms are often utilized by spiritualistic groups for a variety of energy healing treatments.

A poor discernment of "good" and "bad" is observed in the realm of elementals. For this reason, it is common to witness the deliberate use of their energy in low magic rituals that intend to harm others. It is hence recommended that fluids conjured from elementals be used with discretion by witchcraft amateurs, as they can be severely destructive for the summoners themselves.

The spiritual element typically named "ether" is a subtle semiphysical fluid, known for giving life force to incarnated beings. The etheric body of animals and humans is nearly all composed of ether, in different frequencies and densities.

The term *ether,* also written as *aether,* was adopted from ancient Greek philosophy and science. Cofounder of the Theosophical Society Madame Blavatsky used the term to correspond with *akasha,* and English authors in the early 1900s also coined the terms *etheric body* and *etheric plane* from the teachings of Theosophy.

Despite the concept of angels being closely identified with Abrahamic religions, which, according to Brown (1849, 521), refer to them as messengers of God, an angel can be any spiritually immaculate and benevolent being who serves as an intermediary between the divine and spiritual realms. Along these lines, the elementals of ether might perhaps be considered angels in the realm of elementals.

Because the Earth's elements are physical, their elementals live in the space between the physical and astral dimensions. However, "ether" is a semiphysical element; as such, its elementals dwell in-between the etheric and astral dimensions.

The elementals of ether will typically remain in the spiritual realms, without ever migrating to any primitive sort of life in the third dimension. That is, ether is not a physical element like earth, water, air, and fire; therefore, ether does not prepare its elementals for an eventual migration to the kingdoms of the physical plane—that is, aquatic, aerial, igneous, plant, and animal. They may, however, incarnate in other dimensions other than the physical third dimension.

It is crucial to emphasize that elementals are embryonic forms of spirits who may eventually migrate to other kingdoms. The migration occurs either to physical beings on Earth—if they pertain to earthly elements—or to other astral and spiritual realms, if they pertain to ether. The migration of spiritual currents from one element to another develops gradually and by physical proximity. For instance, etheric waves of stones that accumulate forms of mosses or undergrowth on their surface tend to enter the plant kingdom through the proximity between the two objects, which etherically mingle over time. Subsequently, the waves that were once part of the stone gradually

Fig. 7.3: The etheric currents of rocks typically migrate to other more complex realms in their physical proximity. Etherically speaking, moss is a primitive transition of etheric currents of an element—such as earth, a stone, or an aggregate of minerals—into the plant kingdom. Illustration by David Barreto.

adapt to life in the plant kingdom. The stone, however, must be in its terminal period of "life," which can be observed when it presents natural deterioration of its molecules. Such a process continues ceaselessly, and so the final results take from hundreds to thousands of years to appear.

The energies of plants that had earlier etheric existences as stones are, commonly, plants correlated to telluric frequencies—that is, plants that act on very materialistic affairs. Likewise, there are fire-related plants, which have conserved the fiery energies of ancestral volcanic rocks and minerals. Rue is an example of a fire-related plant; fern is related to water; and rosemary is akin to air.

The etheric currents of an entire mountain may migrate to the trees that cover it. The migration of waves and etheric currents may be imagined as thermal conduction. Thermal conduction is "the diffusion of thermal energy (heat) within one material or between objects in contact" (Energy Education Encyclopedia n.d.). According to the second law of thermodynamics, energy (heat) will flow from the hot environment to the cold one in an attempt to equalize the temperature difference (Bird, Stewart, and Lightfoot 2007, 266).

Eventually, the etheric currents of plants and trees migrate to insects who live collectively. Subsequently, the ether currents of insects migrate to larger, more individualized insects, and later to small reptiles and amphibians. The currents of ether customarily develop a more complex structure each time they reach a different realm.

The complexity of certain elements can be investigated based upon its interaction with the surrounding environment.

Mountains, rocks, and an aggregate of minerals, are normally under sunlight and rain, continuously interacting with the energies of light and water. However, they still interact little with their surroundings, exhibiting a slow migration to other realms.

Oceans, rivers, and bodies of water interact with other elements directly: minerals infuse in water, light agitates it, and gases merge with it. Water also changes into different states: liquid as water, solid as ice, and gas as vapor. It also circulates in the bodies of all living beings.

The migration of water's etheric currents develops through thousands of years, albeit at a much faster rate than stones and aggregates of minerals do.

Air assembles a layer of gases that comprise the atmosphere of the Earth. Air is thus retained by the Earth's gravity, surrounding the planet and forming its planetary atmosphere. The composition of outer space primarily consists of hydrogen and helium, yet it remains a vacuum environment. Gases in this space are dispersed as scattered matter. (If this interests you, Baird 2013 has great answers on all things science.) The basic elements of creation on Earth are limited to those found within the Earth's atmosphere. Photons from the sun originate outside of Earth's atmosphere, however, they penetrate through the atmosphere and become integrated into terrestrial existence.

Plants and trees not only interact with the elements—they also combine, transport, and transform them. A tree incorporates underground minerals and water while absorbing luminosity and gases from aboveground. Therefore, trees assist in the migration of telluric and aquatic ethers from their roots and aerial and igneous ethers from their leaves by propelling the basic elementary energies to experience more variation of states. The interaction of a plant or tree with the environment is rather active, which designates their ethereal energy as the closest to that of the animal kingdom.

The migration of ethers from one realm to the other occurs during life, not solely at the time of "death." Elements, as well as plants and insects, do not have a structured soul; instead, they are endowed with etheric currents that sustain their lives. In this case, migration of ether (subtle energy) is less complex than the reincarnation of a spirit—hence it unfolds gradually during life.

It is crucial to accentuate that not every single animal, plant, or elemental will necessarily follow the path described—nonetheless, most less complex beings on Earth do. It is, likewise important to emphasize that when currents of ether migrate from an element or object to another, other exterior currents occupy the spaces "left behind." Thus, evolution evolves alongside the migration cycle of ethers from realm to realm endlessly.

## GUARDIAN ANIMALS
## IN THE CELTIC TRADITION

The belief in animal spirit guides and animal guardians remains common to a number of animistic cultures and religions around the world. Unlike zoolatry, where animals are deities and numerous gods receive sacrifices, animal guides and animal guardians are normally seen as friendly beings who appear to rescue or support an individual or group of individuals in their journeys.

In Celtic traditions, the behavior of certain animals is seen as omens, and various deities are strongly associated with local animals. According to Berresford (1998, 175), the Celtic word for bear became the name of Artio, the bear goddess, and the Celtic word for horse, Epona, became the name of the equine goddess.

In the Celtic locales, animals were also viewed as part of spirituality based on their characteristics. For example, stags, which shed and regrow antlers throughout their lives, suggested growth cycles. Beavers were seen to be skillful workers in wood. Snakes were seen as guardians of long and eternal life, for being able to renew themselves by shedding their skin. Animals were revered for having qualities and abilities that humans did not (Green 1992).

The animals seen as guardians were typically envoys of the god to which those animals were related. At times, people thought that the animal was the divine in animal form. The Celts typically sought the blessings of their gods before going hunting and, as a means of atonement for their act of taking wildlife from the natural environment, performed sacrifices using domestic animals. Hunting was perceived as both a symbolic and practical activity, as the shedding of blood was believed to not only result in the death of the animal, but also to nourish and renew the earth (Green 2005).

In European pagan folklore, animals of power and animal spirits are two concepts that have interchangeably evoked interpretations of a magical being. Nevertheless, an animal of power is usually physical, whereas the animal spirit unfolds as the spirit of an animal, intuition, or the appearance of an animal-like specter.

It can be suggested that, unlike the animals of totems, which are summoned for their specific abilities and as a fleeting source of inspiration, the animals in Celtic culture would appear unexpectedly when an individual truly needed them. Conversely, the Celts and Druids viewed the appearance of certain animals as a powerful omen and a message from the spirits of the supernatural, either beneficial or of bad luck, so several species were feared and avoided (Green 1992). Animals were believed to possess abilities to teach and knowledge to share. Consequently, their appearance was most likely seen as a signal for the Celts to connect with their purpose in life. Unlike the selection of totem animals, the Celtic animal would choose the individual, appearing only when they were ready to embrace its symbols and wisdom.

Each living being has been generated by a specific frequency of Source—hence, every animal includes a different facet of the divine. As the black tourmaline correlates to rue, which correlates to snakes, the same divine essence is observed in all three species. Along these lines, the animal spirit that shows itself portrays the symbolism of that divine essence in which it was created. This regards apparition experienced in meditative and unconscious states, as well as in dreams.

Overall, most manifestations of guardian animals occur in meditation visualizations and in dreams rather than in the material world. Simply seeing an animal in the material world does not mean that messages are being given from a guardian or from the heavens whatsoever. Animals do exist on this planet to evolve in their own worlds and not merely as a result of the existence of humans.

## FAMILIARS

Laynton (2013) states that in European folklore of the medieval period, familiars assisted witches in their magical practices. A familiar would often appear as an animal. They were described as clearly defined, in three-dimensional shapes, in vivid colors, and lively with movement and sound by those who claim to have come into contact with them (Wilby 2005).

According to Willis (1995) folklore holds that familiar spirits, also known as imps, were kept in containers such as pots or baskets. These entities were said to be sustained by milk, bread, beer, and pieces of meat. However, it was believed that these spirits had an insatiable thirst for the blood of the witch who kept them.

Familiars were also considered malevolent or benevolent, depending on whom they were serving. Familiars working for witches, often to provide protection and appearing via incantation, were categorized as demons; familiars working for ordinary humans were more often categorized as fairies.

Modern witchcraft practitioners, symbolically adopt pets and wildlife as a means to manifest the ancestral tradition of having a "magical animal" nearby.

Fig. 7.4. A 1579 English illustration of a
witch feeding her familiars.

# ARCHETYPES

Archetypes are preconceived ideas regarding the symbolic and literal characteristics of something. In the case of animals, they concern, among other elements, their natural abilities, personality traits of entire species, and their admirable instincts.

As explained by Carl Jung in *Man and His Symbols* (1964, 107), the collective unconscious is "the part of the psyche that retains and transmits the common psychological inheritance of mankind." Ideas, in turn, are actually how individuals unconsciously interpret all that exists, and they are usually experienced as mental representational images of an object or an abstract concept. One view on the nature of ideas, also called innate ideas, is that they could not have arisen as a representation of an object of perception but rather were, in some sense, always present. These are distinguished from adventitious ideas, which are images or concepts accompanied by the judgment that they are caused or occasioned by an external object. (For more on ideas and innate ideas, see Locke 1689.)

Another view, as explained in the *The Encyclopedia of Philosophy*, holds that ideas are only discovered in the same way that the real world is discovered: from individual experiences (Borchert 2006). All confusion about the way ideas arise is in part due to the use of the term *idea* to cover both represented perceptions and the object of conceptual thought. This can be illustrated in terms of the scientific doctrines of innate ideas and "concrete ideas versus abstract ideas." In this manner, ideas can either involve the perception of an object and abstract concepts, as well as the theorizing of an intention and suggestion. Therefore, archetypes are the primary ideas of all that exists in the collective consciousness.

The understanding of archetypes commonly connects to Jungian archetypes and to Plato's theory of ideas. In Plato's theory, the material world is not as real or as authentic compared to timeless, absolute, unchangeable ideas.

Carl Jung (1969) equivalently theorized that universal, archaic symbols and images that derive from the collective unconscious are the psyche's counterpart of instinct. His theory of archetypes is described as a sort of innate nonspecific knowledge, acquired from the aggregate of human history, which prefigures and directs conscious behavior. Just as the human body is a museum with regard to the long history of its genes, so is the psyche.

Jung (1969) also described archetypes as impressions of important or frequently recurring situations from the distant human past. He suggested that as our ancestors, and ourselves, have experienced a given idea several times, it settles in our unconscious mind, able to emerge should a first contact with the archetype occur. Jung would conventionally correlate animal archetypes to representations of people's inner self, affirming that they would reflect hidden instincts—hence the use of creatures in numerous myths, which serve as lessons regarding human ego.

In an initial definition of the term, Carl Jung (1960, 137–38) wrote: "Archetypes are typical modes of apprehension and, wherever we find uniform and regularly recurring modes of apprehension, we are dealing with an archetype, regardless of whether its mythological character is recognized or not." He traces the term back to Philo, Irineu, and Corpus Hermeticum, who associate archetypes with the division and the creation of the world; and also notes the close relationship with Platonic ideas (Singer 1968, 36–37). These archetypes inhabit a world beyond the chronology of human life, developing on an evolutionary time scale.

Archetypes of animals as symbols and emblems observed in most world religions and folklore may also be described as the totality of experiences of people, which configures the interpretation of reality.

For example, when a thought about an apple arises, the subsequent ideas are of sweetness, the feminine, love, sex, and mysticism. When a thought about gold arises, the ideas that follow are of wealth, luxury, prosperity, shine, and royalty. Thoughts on the moon are followed by ideas of mystery, night, femininity, intuition, and magic. Thoughts of New York bring the ideas of lights, greatness, conquest, power, and modernity.

Besides rendering a conscious meaning, archetypes act for the perfection of the idea or concept approached. In the case of an apple, its archetype invariably is of a luminous red, round, large, glossy, and appetizing fruit.

Some cultures believe that frogs represent prosperity. However, in the collective conscious of the world, frogs may also connote witchcraft and swamps. Therefore, it is crucial to perceive archetypes globally, not just locally. Intelligence and technology are examples of abstract concepts. The thought of intelligence invariably brings with it the idea of the genius, wisdom, success, and the prodigy. Technology, in turn, summons the idea of futurism, innovative machinery, and precision tools.

Ultimately, the archetype is an idealized and contemplative idea of an object or abstract concept. A painting of Jesus Christ may be consciously interpreted as "divine" by a Christian and, contrarily, considered "vague" by an agnostic. However, the collective conscious where the archetype of Jesus Christ is stationed results in the same response for both the individuals: pacifism; compassion; suffering; and sanctification. This unconscious idea of Jesus Christ occurs as both the Christian and the agnostic individuals interpret that character as an idealized idea or concept. Although the agnostic individual may perceive Jesus as a fictional character, the archetype of such a figure does not depend on physical evidence as an agent for validation. Therefore, Jesus Christ is conceptualized equally by all.

To better understand how unconscious ideas overrun conscious ideas, the examples of well-known story characters of literature may help—for instance, Snow White. Despite being a fictional character, the archetype of such a personality is universally established as that of an innocent, gentle, and joyous young lady. For human minds, it's not important whether the character pertains to a physical or nonmaterial idea. Thus, a film or fairy tale character is as real as historical human characters, like Napoleon Bonaparte or Mahatma Gandhi.

Archetypes are based on the strength of the collective conscious. In other words, an individual whose judgment on such a symbol differs from that of the collective conscious is still thoroughly influenced by the latter. The presence (and consequently the image) of animals has a direct impact on the lives of humans, by triggering instant emotional reactions. The idea of an animal, in particular, connotes the essence they depict.

The assimilation of an animal archetype through their image diverges from what is known as "subliminal stimuli," which are any sensory stimuli below an individual's threshold for conscious perception (Greenwald, Klinger, and Schuh 1995). Subliminal stimuli and their affairs depend on the conscious mind directly, as they interact with what can be cognitively assimilated by the individual in a lifetime. On the other hand, archetypes are preestablished ideas that do not depend on one's cognition. Therefore, archetypes are perceived by the unconscious minds, as opposed to what is perceived as subliminal stimuli by the subconscious mind.

Given the power of archetypes, trademarks, company logos, supermarket products, and symbols on clothing and ornaments deliberately and openly influence people, albeit less discourteously than subliminal messages attempt to do. Moreover, certain archetypes have groups of spirits associated to them. These entities typically ally themselves with a particular symbol and, therefore, connect their minds to such archetypes, including those of animals.

Archetypes are related to dualism, which is a philosophy that assumes that the human being is composed of material and immaterial elements. Thus, the existence of archetypes is independent of the conscious mind, the thalamus, or the prefrontal cortex, although the conscious mind can considerably influence and be influenced by the archetypes. Archetypes are immaterial ideals, like mental holograms stationed in layers of dimensions related to the unconscious mind.

When archetypes are deliberately used in marketing, businesses, and products, they maintain consumers and observers in a specific emotional stance, by delivering from the unconscious mind to the conscious mind all the sentimental meaning an archetype may hold. Neurotransmitters, which are the chemical messengers produced by nerve cells (Lodish, Berk, and Zipursky 2000), are discharged in the body as a consequence.

After the production of certain neurotransmitters and hormones, the individual experiences feelings related to what emotion the archetypes conduct. This happens from the collective conscious to the conscious mind, and finally materializes as feelings and behavior. The effects of an archetype on the individual are, thus, the result of extraphysical and biologic processes that are inescapably complementary to one another.

By encountering an archetype, which is not only portrayed by images, but also as sound, taste, smell, or general abstract concepts, neural association occurs in the brain. The neural association occurs when an idea intertwines with another, regardless of how compatible or similar they are. For example, an elegantly dressed woman who appears in an advertisement for a casino donates those archetypes of seductive power and desire to the brand. As such, by neural association, observers may attribute such qualities to the casino, as the association between the woman and the brand is established in the brain. When the advertisement catches the individual's attention, the model in it is attractive enough that the individual pays less attention to their surrounding environment and even to their principles concerning gambling. This is because ideas of seductive power and desire activate the brain's reward system.

The reward system is a group of brain structures responsible for motivation and positive emotions, such as pleasure (Schultz, 2015). This system motivates behavior by influencing individuals to engage in activities that lead to pleasurable sensations, like eating tasty food, or playing video games, and to avoid unpleasant tasks like cleaning. Repetition of these pleasurable activities can lead to mild addiction and the preference for activities that release more dopamine. This process can reduce interest in activities that do not provide as much dopamine release.

Experimental psychologists make clear distinctions between "wanting" something and "liking" something, where dopamine appears to be important for "wanting," but not necessarily for "liking" (Berridge and Robinson 2016). When a dopamine rush activates the reward system, the individual's attention and focus are on the potential reward. In this case, the reward is not an interaction with the model in the ad for the casino, but the desire to experience more of what was experienced when the ad was first seen. Therefore, the archetype of an elegantly dressed model is stronger than that of other casinos that do not use such powerful associative marketing. Ultimately, that casino uses the archetype of vanity and lust to propel a neural association between the casino itself with potential consumers' brain areas that demand considerable amounts of dopamine, which may lure more clients.

The archetypes of animals have an explicitly similar effect. However, the concepts carried by the various animals, also popular in advertising and logos, are abstract ideas, such as vitality, heightened skills, and peace.

Archetype of animals work as symbols, images, and ideas. Thus, seeing a real animal or having a specific animal at home will not serve the subconscious mind as an archetype, as the mind expects an idealized idea of them. An archetype generally incorporates all the main qualities of the object, not just the ones assumed as "positive" aspects. Parrots, for instance, which can be considered eloquent, have an archetype constituted by connotations of gossip, imitation, and limited movement; elephants, bearer of incredible memory, exhibits traces of slowness; and white doves, a symbol of peace, may as well carry connotations of forced servitude, captivity and even cheap tricks, due to their recent use by audience magicians. In the company of doves, hens correlate to motherly love; however, as a result of the meat industry, their archetype is currently shifting into unfortunate ideas of stress and apathy. Nevertheless, in the Age of Aquarius, due to commence approximately in 2150 CE, such an archetype will be entirely returned to its original aspect—that of love and motherhood.

## ALCHEMY

Animals were metaphors for alchemical aspects, elements, and their stages. Werness (2006) explains that eagles that fly high represented the volatile ammonia; red lizards represented the crimson-colored cin-

nabar; and wolves, most of whom were gray, represented silvery anti-
mony. Serpents were related to the transmigration of the soul (for their
skin-sloughing); hence they were the symbol supporting the alchemist
who spiritually ascended.

Hermes Trismegistus, a syncretic combination of the Greek god
Hermes and the Egyptian god Thoth, was the purported author of texts
that formed the basis of Hermeticism. The legendary figure is frequently
depicted carrying a staff, known as the caduceus, with two coiled serpents around it. Metaphorically, the object was used to demonstrate
his power and ability to transform his own shape. Frothingham (1916)
argued that the staff or wand entwined by two snakes represented the
god Hermes in the preanthropomorphic era.

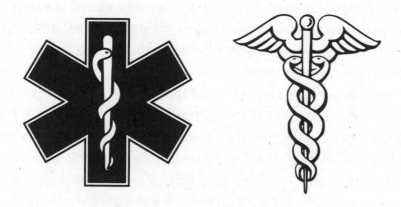

Fig. 7.5. The Asclepius Rod (*left;* symbol of medicine) and
Hermes' caduceus (*right;* symbol of commerce).

In alchemy, the use of mythical creatures as symbols is a common
practice. The dragon, for example, is thought to represent the metal
mercury. It is believed that the dragon symbolizes the four elements of
earth, water, air, and fire through its four legs, scales, wings, and fiery
breath. The three-headed dragon is seen as the philosophers' stone and
elixir for eternal life, which is thought to represent salt, sulfur, and
mercury, or the planets Earth, Jupiter, and Mercury. Some ancient texts

even referred to the dragon as a metaphor for transcending the material world and reaching a higher spiritual state. (See Hauck 1999.)

## MORPHISM

The concept of bi-, tri-, and tetra-morphism in ancient cultures involves the representation of multiple species within a single symbolic unit. Examples of this can be seen in various protective deities of Egyptian, Greek, and Babylonian origin. Additionally, the Egyptian sphinx serves as an interesting example of allegorical morphism.

Following the examples of different elements in one item, the image of the Baphomet reappeared in occult groups in Victorian England. Implicitly, Baphomet was the depiction of the four elements of nature. In its illustrations, opposites complement one another alongside the depiction of a spiritual flame, which symbolizes spiritual control over matter. Baphomet's goat legs symbolize earth, the scales in the abdomen signify water, the wings represent air, and the torch above its head represents fire. The duality between human and animal, as well as male and female, are also present. In the figure can be seen the face of a goat versus the torso of a human, the right arm and breast of a woman versus the left arm and breast of a man, and one of the arms pointing above—a reference to the macro, which diffuses—versus the other arm pointing below, a reference to the micro, which concentrates.

Baphomet as a deity can be traced back to medieval times, when numerous Knights Templar were accused of worshiping him. The name derived from an Old French corruption of the name Mahomet—meaning that the allegedly heretic Templars were worshiping Muhammed, the then anti-Christian character during the Crusades (Stahuljak 2013).

In conclusion, the use of animal symbolism has been prevalent throughout history, serving as powerful emblems in cultures, religions, and philosophies of the past. Encompassing both physical and spiritual elements, animals were often seen as spiritual beings with special attributes and abilities, and their representation has served to embody

Fig. 7.6. Examples of morphism: arts produced in the medieval times, along with 1856's illustration of Baphomet (*top right*). The beasts portray two or more elements of different species in one item.

various divine meanings and purposes. From gods to the power of nature, from religious sacrifice to advertising, their image has played a significant role in shaping human beliefs and values, but nevertheless, their exploitation causes dramatic effects on the energetic body of humans and on Earth.

# PART 3
· · · · · · · · · ·
# THE BRINK OF CONSCIOUS EXPANSION

# 8 Planetary Transformation through the Ages

## THE EXPANSION OF THE UNIVERSE

According to quantum theory, light is constituted of particles called photons (Joos 1951, 679), the carriers of light itself, as well as other types of electromagnetic radiation, such as radio waves. Merriam-Webster's online dictionary defines the electromagnetic spectrum as "the entire range of wavelengths of frequencies of electromagnetic radiation extending from gamma rays to the longest radio waves and including visible light."

Each color in the spectrum has a different wavelength. For example, the red light in the spectrum has a longer wavelength, while the blue light has a shorter wavelength. When an object is in motion, a change in wavelength can be observed, appearing as a modified color of the spectrum. When an object travels toward the observer, its waves appear compressed (bluer), but if it is moving away from the observer, the waves will appear elongated (redder). (Read a good explanation in Andrade 1959.)

In 1912, astronomer Vesto Slipher discovered that light from remote galaxies was red-shifted (see Slipher's 1913 paper), which was later interpreted as galaxies moving away from the Earth. In 1922, Alexander Friedmann used Einstein field equations to provide theoretical evidence that the universe is expanding. (See an online reprint of Friedmann's article published in 1999.) In 1927, Georges Lemaitre independently reached a similar conclusion to Friedmann on a theoretical basis, also presenting the first observational evidence for a linear relationship between distance to galaxies and their recessional velocity. (See Lemaitre's 1931 English translation.) Edwin Hubble's 1929 observations confirmed Lemaitre's findings two years later. This phenomenon that examines the direction of celestial bodies based on the colors they depict is known as the Doppler effect. Assuming such a cosmological principle, these findings, known as Hubble's Law or the Hubble-Lemaitre law, would imply that all galaxies are moving away from one another.

The universe is expanding, and therefore the position of the planet Earth in the universe is never the same in space as time passes. This planet may seem to be in its exact position after an entire orbit around the sun; nevertheless, the sun itself is also moving and so is the Milky Way. Based on numerous observational experiments and theoretical reasoning, the scientific consensus is that space itself is expanding, having initiated its expansion very rapidly, within the first fraction of a second after the Big Bang. This nature of expansion is known as metric expansion. In mathematics and physics, a "metric" means a measure of distance, which implies that the sense of distance within the universe is itself changing. From the perspective of an expanding universe, the Earth will never relocate to the same point in space ever again. It is possible that metric expansion (Hawking 1966) is also progressing on other planes of reality as the fields of consciousness expand their areas of operation to higher levels. As such, there appears to be a link between the evolution or enlightenment of consciousness and the metric expansion of all universes in terms of the moral and intellectual growth on Earth and elsewhere in the universe.

The physical expansion of the universe, galaxies, and solar systems unfolds in cycles, which converge with extraphysical cycles that pertain to the spiritual condition of planets. Thus, understanding how past planetary cycles affected the lives of those who inhabited Earth may provide glimpses of how future eras will manifest.

Planetary cycles follow a scheme where dramatic changes are observed. However, the primary motivators for a local population to change its behavior are altruism and love. In other words, even if an astrological aspect indicates a beneficial and serene period, favorable qualities will only occur if the collective energy of the inhabitants allows it through vibratory affinity. (See Barbault 2016.) In particular, Arroyo (1978) explains that if two different individuals experience the very same astrological transition, the one who is prone to benevolence will experience the fruitful qualities of that aspect. The other individual, however, given his notorious inferiority of principles, will inevitably experience the darkest parts of such an astrological configuration. The same analogy applies to galaxies, regions of a planet, towns, and groups of consciousnesses.

The world did experience the darkest sides of its past astrological eras, for its current population displays flawed ethics and, often, primitive habits.

Widespread atrocities against animals have been witnessed in all previous ages of this planet; nonetheless, as it is expected that the Earth's human inhabitants tend toward a more docile, responsible, and tolerant attitude, the Age of Aquarius will tend to exhibit its best traits, thus promoting a general truce and benefiting animals with well-deserved freedom.

## ASTROLOGICAL AGES

In addition to its diurnal (daily) rotation upon its axis and annual rotation around the sun, the Earth has a precessional motion involving a slow periodic shift of the axis itself: approximately one degree every 72 years. This motion, mostly caused by the moon's gravity, gives rise to the precession of the equinoxes, in which the sun's position on the ecliptic at the time of the vernal equinox gradually changes with time, as it is measured against the background of fixed stars. Simply put, this phenomenon induces what is known as precession of the equinoxes, or the change in the orientation of the Earth's rotation. An equinox is usually counted as the time when the plane of the Earth's equator passes through the geometric center of the solar disc. This occurs twice a year, around March 20 (spring) and September 23 (autumn). (Regarding the equinox, see Furst, 2011.)

In graphic terms, the Earth wobbles like a top, and from Earth's perspective, the constellations appear to move slightly from west to east at a rate of approximately one degree every 72 years. One degree is twice the diameter of the sun or moon as viewed from Earth.

Astrological schools theorize that astrological ages have a significant impact on paradigm shifts in all societies around the world, influencing culture, politics, human migration, and so on. An astrological age is traditionally described as an era when considerable changes are observed, whereby it is marked by the aspects of the sidereal zodiac observed at the time the spring equinox. Because each zodiac sign is comprised of 30 imaginary degrees and the twelve constellations fit within the celestial circumference, each astrological age is believed to last approximately 2,150–2,160 years (72 years × 30 degrees). Along these lines, the sun crosses the equator at the vernal equinox by one degree every 72 years; one whole constellation (on average) every 2,160 years; and all 12 every 25,920* years.

With the earliest fossil evidence of *Homo sapiens,* archaeological findings comprehensively propose that the first modern humans appeared in Africa around 300,000–200,000 years ago (Scerri et al. 2018). The Upper Paleolithic model theorizes that modern human behavior arose through abrupt cognitive and genetic changes in the continent. Klein (1995) proposes that these behaviors changed approximately 40,000–50,000 years ago. Other models, however, such as McBrearty and

---

*The 25,920-year cycle, as well as the 2,150–2,160-year duration of each astrological age and the approximate change of precession of equinoxes moving one degree every 72 years, are midpoint calculations. The variation of the beginning and the ending of ages is proportionately based on algebraic estimates, which were examined by several astronomers and cosmologists. The use of such dates in this work is built on the average of the dates surveyed—therefore, it does not reflect ultra-precise dates. Hence, the dates may vary slightly in the following paragraphs. The discrepancy, however, is negligible, considering it does not surpass ten years in each astrological age length.

Brooks (2000), focus on how modern human behavior may have arisen through gradual steps, approximately 70,000–100,000 years ago.

Despite attempts to leave Africa, which may have started around 250,000 years ago, the earliest evidence of modern humans via the "out-of-Africa" migration dates back to 150,000 years ago (Harvati et al. 2019). Nevertheless, most of the early waves of migration out of the continent appear to have not been very successful until around 100,000 years ago. The period of the first successful out-of-Africa migration occurred around 80,000 years ago (Spier 2010).

Typical traits of modern human civilizations, such as agriculture, only appeared in Eurasia approximately 12,000–10,000 years ago (Zeder 2011), and human societies only completely transitioned to sedentary agriculture approximately 10,000 years ago in the Fertile Crescent (Tudge 1998)—a region that comprises modern-day Iraq, Syria, Lebanon, Israel, Palestine, Jordan, Egypt, and portions of Turkey and Iran. The records of those first settlements unveil the development of agriculture, writing, villages, and even the domestication of dogs, later contributing to the emergence of early settled civilizations from approximately 4500 BCE, initially appearing in Mesopotamia and starting along with the Bronze Age (Noble et al. 2013).

Placed on archaeological findings and anthropological research, conjointly with the investigation of the history of modern humans, this chapter attempts to construct an analogy between the history of the civilizations and the astrological ages, assessing their congruence. The aim is to trace a parallel of remarkable shifts in paradigm, such as culture, society, and politics—and verify the affinity of such eras with the perspective of astrological theology, which claims astrological ages play a pivotal role in the unfolding of these time periods.

Nevertheless, the changing of astronomical eras, which is observed in every celestial orbit, is not equal to the previous ones under the same constellations. The cosmological ages never repeat themselves exactly as they were before, as the planet resides, during each age, in a different locale of space-time.

### Age of Leo: 10,750 BCE to 8600 BCE

The first settled civilization in history was the Sumerians, from 4500 BCE. Nevertheless, it is pivotal to first appraise the Age of Leo, which came before the Sumerians, for it shaped the world with an altered climate, vegetation, and redefinition of coastal landscapes that made it possible for the first tribes to evolve into civilizations.

The Age of Leo, astrologically ruled by the sun, was the first age where the Earth had emerged from the last glacial period, which ended approximately 11,700 years ago (Walker et al. 2009; Rapp 2009). The Age of Leo also covered the final period of the Paleolithic Era.

During the Age of Leo the planet, and most prominently the Levant region, were favored by the sun's warmth and luminosity, which allowed the pioneering of the first agricultural way of living. This gave rise to cultures identified as Neolithic, first appearing in the tenth millennium BCE (Bellwood 2004, 384). Those primitive, albeit structured cultures, drew their last breath during the Age of Virgo—a methodical earthy period that prompted modern humanity to move into a future of farming and acculturation.

Due to changes in Earth's atmosphere (Rapp 2009), numerous species of animals disappeared during the Age of Leo, while others flourished. The event may be presumed to have been responsible for the spiritual evolution and migration of spirits from one species into others (Xavier 1939a). The occurrence equally affected the plant kingdom and that of humans, the climate being the pillar around which plant, animal, and human communities revolve.

### Age of Cancer: 8600 BCE to 6450 BCE

After the melting of the ice sheets that used to cover a substantial part of the northern hemisphere, sea levels rose, remolding all lands across the globe. That process caused sudden shifts in the configuration of coastlines, new irrigation systems, submersion and the merging of lands, salination of lakes, areas of freshwater, and a general alteration in regional weather patterns on a temporary but also large scale (Andersen and Borns 1997).

In astrological theology, Cancer is classified as a water sign, which associates the constellation with bodies of water, irrigation and, in particular, with emotions that relate to family identity and the home. The Cancerian constellation thus enhanced the idea of the family unit and was connected to the concept of family members living in the same dwellings—like huts—separated from the other individuals of the tribe. Thereby, the building of rudimentary houses began, marking the peak of the Neolithic Era (Meyer 2106). During the Age of Cancer, the regions of Phoenicia, Assyria, Mesopotamia, and Lower Egypt experienced the Earth's first proto-civilizations. These civilizations transitioned from nomadic to agricultural, with a more settled way of living that included the domestication of animals and farming (Tudge 1998).

The Age of Cancer marks the first prominent transition that domesticated animals such as dogs and cats experienced, advancing from an exclusively instinctual nature to being affectionate and loyal to another species. In spite of the domestication of dogs starting 6,500 years before that of cats, the relationship between humans and pets as cherished "family members" only occurred from the Age of Cancer onward.

## Age of Gemini: 6450 BCE to 4300 BCE

The written history of humanity was preceded by its prehistory, beginning in the Paleolithic Era and followed by the Neolithic Era. During the Geminian era, ruled by the planet Mercury, the structure of language developed as never occurred before.

Proto-civilizations started to revolve around barter, or an exchange of food items—including wheat, barley, lentils, beans, onions, and milk—done without the need for money or currency (Johnson 2017). Animals or their flesh were rarely bartered during this period. This practice may have triggered the development of a writing system, as individuals had to name and account for their rustic manner of producing and exchanging. Writing and grammar systems also flourished at this time. As the Age of Cancer emphasized emotional bonding, Gemini promoted exchange and communication, thus generating an intellectually complex civilization.

The interchange between humans and companion animals, like dogs and cats, also began during this period, making animals partially responsible for the formation of the first civilizations, such as the Sumerians, who would emerge during the Age of Gemini and go on to flourish during the Age of Taurus.

## Age of Taurus: 4300 BCE to 2150 BCE

The Age of Taurus, which followed that of Gemini, was the apotheosis for the development of modern agriculture and the need for settlement, which marked the pivotal beginning of the first civilizations on Earth in Mesopotamia.

The Sumerians were the earliest known civilization in the historical region of Lower Mesopotamia, emerging during the early Bronze Age and reaching their height as a complex civilization from 4500 BCE to 1900 BCE.

Some believe that the migration of spirits from other planets, who possessed far more advanced human traits and knowledge than the spirits of those already inhabiting the planet, propelled this civilization forward. According to one of Spiritism's most celebrated pieces of literature (Xavier and Emmanuel 1939b), this was the period when most exiled humanoid spirits from other orbs began to populate the Earth, incarnating in human bodies. Once incarnated amid the first civilizations, these spirits could bring more elevated characteristics to human societies (Xavier and Emmanuel, 1939b). Along these lines, the Sumerians were the first humans to acquire contemporaneous rational behavior.

Sumerian farmers grew an abundance of crops, which enabled them to form urban settlements. Thus, modern agriculture promoted settlement, which led individuals to desist from the nomadic venturing, typical of proto-civilizations. Thereafter, habitation, plantation, and animal agriculture flourished, and the accumulated produce was often used as a commodity—a distinct Taurean method of ruling via economical means. The Mesopotamian shekel became one of the world's first currencies. In this period, currency made of rare metals or pieces of adorned wood or stones also served to represent money.

Although the Sumerians were the first civilization on Earth, other societies similarly blossomed in the Age of Taurus, notably the Norte Chico (modern Peru) and the Minoan (Greek islands), as well as those of ancient Egypt, China, Mesoamerica, and the Indus Valley.

The Indus Valley civilization emerged during the last quarter of the Age of Taurus, starting between 3300 BCE and 1900 BCE in what today is Pakistan and northwestern India. The civilization was noted for its urban development, building methods utilizing brick, and innovations in water supply and drainage. The Indus Valley was the most widespread civilization in the world during that period of history.

The Age of Taurus also involved the development of religion.

Apis, the ox deity, was the god of fertility in the Egyptian pantheon. Linked to the king's power, the bull was the most important of the sacred animals in ancient Egypt from the Second Dynasty to the New Kingdom (Levenda 2020). According to Judeo-Christian tradition, the golden calf also began to be worshipped during this age: when Moses ascended to Mount Sinai to receive God's Ten Commandments, the people of Israel, tired of waiting for Moses and God, forced Aaron to create an idol that they would worship instead (Exodus 32: 1–5).

In terms of religious slaughter, some of the earliest archaeological

Fig. 8.1. Egyptian statuette of Apis. Late Period, 664–343 BCE. The Metropolitan Museum, New York. Gift of J. Pierpont Morgan, 1917.

evidence suggests that the practice first started in ancient Egypt. The oldest Egyptian burial sites containing animal remains originate from the Badari culture of Upper Egypt, which flourished between 4400 and 4000 BCE (Flores 1999). Animal sacrifices for the deities and pagan gods endured until Egypt became a Roman province (30 BCE–641 CE).

Written religious history began with the invention of writing itself, approximately 3200 BCE (Nissen, Damerow, and Englund 1993). The invention of writing replaced reliance on spoken language with a more sophisticated method of naming and counting goods. Prehistoric proto-writing dates back to before 3000 BCE. The earliest texts come from the cities of Uruk and Jemdet Nasr, dating between 3500 BCE and 3000 BCE (Nissen, Damerow, and Englund 1993).

As a structured civilization, the Sumerians and their immediate neighbors promoted the advance of construction, design, and detailed reporting for the first time. Lower Egypt also saw its influence grow.

The Egyptian civilization emerged during this ultra-materialistic period. Its pyramids were erected during the Age of Taurus, and techniques revolving around geometry also flourished. Like no other place Egypt promulgated the concept of luxury, elaborate ornaments, and the emphasis on guaranteeing a prosperous and secure life after death. Correlated to astrological theology, Taurus's concerns revolve around security, stability, and preservation. Temples, jewelry, and colossal tombs were reflections of the planet Venus's tendency for luxurious excess.

Overall, agriculture—a science closely related to Taurus—was accompanied by standardized writing and the arts, aesthetics, and the accumulation of goods, making this an era that established control via economic power.

## Age of Aries: 2150 BCE to 1 CE

In the Age of Aries, control by military power subdued Taurus's control by economic power. Civilizations founded on Taurus (earth) suffered a decline, while those of Aries (fire) gained ground. What was built in Taurus was later conquered and raided in Aries, with barbarian invasions and conquest occurring in most of the northern hemisphere.

Numerous civilizations also emerged in all corners of the planet during this period.

In the Age of Aries, human and animal sacrifice became a notable part of worship in the Aztec culture, and the Aztecs bred dogs, eagles, jaguars, and deer. Dogs were often sacrificed en masse, especially to the god Xototl. Similar to Anubis and his association with dogs digging up graves, Xototl, the Aztec god of fire and lightening, was commonly depicted as a dog-headed being. (The Florentine Codex, by Bernardino de Sahagun [1577], remains a good source regarding pre-Columbian America.) During the ten days preceding the festival of Izcalli, various animals would be captured by the people, to be thrown into the fire on the night of celebration (Roy 2005). The cult of the god Quetzalcoatl required the sacrifice of butterflies and hummingbirds (Nguyen 2016).

The rise of civilizations in Greece also occurred during the Age of Aries. The Mycenaean Civilization, which spanned from 1600 BCE to 1100 BCE (Demand 1996), was marked by its skilled warriors and seafarers. They established a network of palace-centered states across the Aegean Sea. Following the collapse of the Mycenaeans came the Greek Dark Ages, lasting from 1100 BCE to 800 BCE (Thommen 2012).

The Roman Kingdom (753 BCE–509 BCE) gave rise to the combative Roman Republic (509 BCE–27 BCE), which expanded its hegemony over the entire Mediterranean Sea. Rosenstein and Morstein-Marx (2006) explain that in this age, the image of the wise priest or elderly figure as a leader receded with the awakening of the younger, stubborn, and masculine archetype, due to its focus on the ideal of *virtus* or the character and duty of the Roman citizen. This ideal emphasized the importance of civic duty, military courage, and the pursuit of justice, which helped to shape the culture of the Republic and set it apart from the more passive and corrupt monarchy that preceded it. Typical Arian characteristics were also evident with systematic law-making, standardized hierarchies, division of classes, and castes and corrections for "order."

As an example of how aggressive punishment became normal, Hammurabi, the sixth king of the First Babylonian Dynasty (1792 BCE to 1750 BCE) issued the Code of Hammurabi, which was one of the first laws to emphasize physical punishment of the perpetrator.

The Code of Hammurabi and the Law of Moses in the Old Testament share numerous similarities. Despite being written between 1200 BCE and 165 BCE (Barton 1998), during the Age of Aries, the stories recorded in the Old Testament usually depict the previous period in history (Coogan 2009)—that is, the Age of Taurus. It is also observed that, despite telling stories of the Age of Taurus, the Old Testament is intrinsically vindictive, a common trait of fiery Aries when in its negative aspect. The implacable personality of God may be observed in several narratives of the Old Testament, such as when Adam and Eve are expelled from Eden to a hostile land as a punishment. This allegory may be theorized as the exile of spirits from Capella* (the brightest star in the Auriga constellation) to planet Earth.

An astrological age may also be lightly influenced by its opposite zodiac sign. As the opposite zodiac sign to Aries is Libra, duality was also prominently observed in that period. As a consequence, laws established across Middle Eastern civilizations, such as the Code of Hammurabi (Roth 1997), and those of the Hittites (Hoffner 1997), implemented provisions for due process, such as the right to a fair trial, the right to confront witnesses, and the obligation of the accuser to provide evidence. In Egypt's New Kingdom, the concept of Ma'at, referring to truth, balance, and justice, was the basis for the presumption of innocence (Karenga [1994] 2003). In Greece, the laws of Solon in the sixth century BCE instituted the presumption of innocence, establishing the right to a fair trial and stating that an accused person is presumed innocent until proven guilty (Leão and Rhodes 2016).

Highlighting the creation of amnesty and balance of Libra, in

---

*Xavier and Emmanuel (1939b) explain that in their native world, the Capellians were jubilant beings. However, some were somewhat hostile toward one another, therefore compromising harmony among the benevolent spirits. Thereupon, a compulsory spiritual exodus occurred, so Earth could benefit from the intellectual advancement of such newcomer spirits, at the same time that those same spirits would polish their appreciation and empathy in Earth's torrid modern times.

1259 BCE the first peace treaty was created between Egypt and Hatti (Anatolia and the Kingdom of Hattusa, modern-day Turkey). Archaeologists found the treaty's original inscriptions in both Egyptian and Hittite versions. The Hittite version is, exceptionally, told in the Bible as the Treaty of Alliance between Hattusili, King of the Hittites and the Pharaoh Ramesses II of Egypt (Langdon and Gardiner 1920).

During this age, men mastered metal more than ever before, leading to this era ruled by Mars being called the Iron Age (Waldbaum 1978). The smelting of iron weaponry replaced that of bronze casting. Iron swords, crafted for the first time, replaced the heavy and warping swords of the Taurean Bronze Age, enhancing military eminence.

In China, numerous dynasties ruled during the Age of Aries, including, in consecutive order, the Xia, Shang, Zhou, and Qin Dynasty, all known for their weaponry inventions and protective wall-building (Eberhard 1941).

The Age of Taurus was a period of polytheism; however, in the Age of Aries a possible inclination toward monotheism emerged in the concept of Brahman. Since the sixth century BCE, Zoroastrians have believed in the supremacy of one God above all: Ahura Mazda, known as the "Maker of All." (This can be found in the collection of primary texts known as the Avesta. See the Ahunuvaiti Gatha, yasna 31, verse 8.) Between 1353–1336 BCE, ceremonial monotheism took its first steps in Egypt with Akhenaten's Great Hymn to the Aten (Ridley 2019). However, subsequent rulers returned to the traditional polytheistic religion and the pharaohs associated with atheism were erased from Egyptian records.

The statuaries of bulls (Taurus) were gradually being replaced by those of the ram (Aries) in this period. Interestingly, in a narrative in the Old Testament, Moses destroyed the golden calf when he led the Israelites out of Egypt (Exodus 32: 1–5).

In the Old Testament, human sacrifices were rare, but did exist. For instance, in the book of Kings, the King of Moab gives his firstborn son and heir as an offering. In the book of Genesis, Abraham presents his son Isaac as a sacrifice to God on Mount Moriah. Abraham obeys, and an angel stops Abraham at the last moment. A ram is sacrificed instead. This may symbolize the Age of Aries (the ram), but biblical scholars have suggested this story's origin was a remembrance of an era when human sacrifice was abolished in favor of animal sacrifice (Stager and Wolff 1984). It is widely agreed that, at the coming of the Age of Pisces, the book of Hebrews 10:10 declared that neither human nor animal sacrifice was needed thereafter, as Jesus had been the final sacrifice. It is also believed that the place of Isaac's binding, Moriah, later became Jerusalem, the city of Jesus's future crucifixion (Goodman, Cohen, and Sorkin 2002).

Fig. 8.2. *The Ghent Alterpiece: Adoration of the Mystic Lamb.* Hubert and Jan van Eyck, 1432. The lamb is said to be a reference to Christ's sacrifice.

## The Age of Pisces: 1 CE to 2150 CE

The Age of Pisces is the embodiment of monotheism, world religions, and control via belief. Sects flourished like never before and sacred symbolism escalated in all civilizations.

According to astrological theology, Pisces is traditionally ruled by Jupiter, a planet commonly associated with the principles of growth and expansion. Contemporaneously, Pisces is ruled by Neptune, a planet associated with illusion and deception when in its negative aspect (Woolfolk 2012). Thus, the two planets presumably are related to delusional religion during this era. Read one way, the expansion and faith of Jupiter multiplied populations and religions in this period, while delusional and escapist Neptune molded them.

After the astronomical discovery of Neptune in 1846, the planet was attributed to Pisces, as it had been named after the Roman god, ruler of the oceans. The name Neptune was given by its discoverer, Urbain Le Verrier, as the planet presents a deep ocean blue color, which prompted the astronomer to connect it to the oceans. The fourteen moons of Neptune were also named after minor sea deities of Roman and Greek mythology.

The central symbol of the Age of Pisces is naturally the fish, which frequently symbolized Jesus Christ in primitive Christianity (contrary to what may be assumed, the cross only became Christianity's main symbol in the fourth century CE according to Allen [1884]).

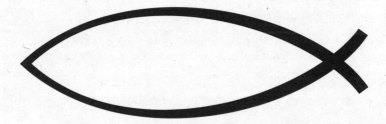

Fig. 8.3. Ichthys. The fish symbol was adopted by early Christians as a secret symbol. Illustration by David Barreto.

Jesus, who is the basis of the New Testament, carries several traits associated with Pisces, such as serenity over anger, which noticeably distanced him from the vengeful god and his rules common in the Old Testament (written during the Age of Aries).

As the most prominent character of the Age of Pisces, Jesus was surrounded by Piscean symbolism across various narratives, such as walking on water (a Piscean element), changing water into wine (a beverage associated with Neptune), washing feet (the body part associated with Pisces), the multiplication of fish, and the twelve apostles, who were nearly all known as fishers.

## Date of the Birth of Jesus
## and the Age of Pisces

Jesus is believed to have been born between 7 and 4 BCE. Consequently, precise dates paralleling the beginning of the Piscean Age and his birth may vary; however, the discrepancy is negligible, considering it does not surpass ten years.

A passage in the Gospel of Matthew 2:1, which may also constitute historical evidence, stated that "Jesus was born in Bethlehem of Judea in the days of King Herod." Such a passage can indicate the exact date of his birth, which supposedly marks the beginning of the Age of Pisces. As a historical event, King Herod died in Jericho in 4 BCE (Schürer 1896, 400–67). Thus, Jesus would have to have been born before Herod's death, since the king would play a significant role in Christ's narratives throughout his life.

In 7 BCE, Jupiter and Saturn were in astronomical conjunction, forming what appeared to be a bright star in the sky, which could be correlated to the Bethlehem Star—the guiding sign for the wise men to find Jesus. Johannes Kepler also considered the claims of the exact year of Jesus's birth and believed that the Star of Bethlehem was a result of a great conjunction. He confirmed this idea by calculating that a triple conjunction of Jupiter and Saturn occurred in 7 BCE (Burke-Gaffney 1937).

As for the pious qualities of Pisces, the vindictive fire of Aries was renewed with the waters of baptism, which replaced the sacrifices and cremation of rams, common among Jews and other religious groups. Mysticism unfolded from practically every ancient religion. Hermeticism was one of the most celebrated esoteric philosophies of the Piscean Age. It refers to the secrets of creation and magic as a natural philosophy and proto-scientific tradition that attempted to purify base metals into gold as well as mature and perfect the soul. Several doctrines used alchemy as a theory of spiritual ascension, or transforming one's consciousness into its more admirable form.

In early Christian and Jewish sects of the first century CE, Gnosticism, which emphasized personal spiritual knowledge (*gnosis*) over the teachings and authority of the church, as well as ritualistic magic and occult sciences, where individuals do not depend on religious norms or tradition, became prominent in countless cultures.

Shame and anger, connected to the shadowy side of Aries, were replaced by Pisces' guilt and pessimism. Among the interminable remorseful and egoistical aberrations of this era, self-flagellation, tithes, indulgences for admission to heaven, and the Inquisition were strongly advocated by religious priests, temples, emperors, and kings. Religion disseminated in this era is characterized by dogmatic rules, where what is taught is imposed by fear and guilt.

One of the negative aspects of Pisces concerns holy wars and conflicts in the name of God. Mass sacrifice for the divine is also a trait of the Piscean negativity. The practice of human sacrifice in the Olmec, Mayan, Teotihuacan, and most infamously, the Aztec cultures is well documented.

Over time emblematically Piscean punishment became common. Long-term prison replaced several acts of public torture and brutal deaths that quenched the thirst of curious mobs during the previous age.

Christians rose to positions of power in the fourth century following the Edict of Milan of 313, as the collapse of centralized authority in Europe gave rise to the Middle Ages (fifth to fifteenth century CE), a period shaped by religious extremism, mass migration, monarchies, superstitions, and astronomy.

The Great Navigations (Age of Discovery) are also qualities of this age, as Pisces rules the deep and vast waters into the unknown.

Subjection and suffering are among the negative qualities of Pisces. Following these lines of reasoning, it is observed that slavery *en masse* was consolidated in all inhabited continents.

Although animal husbandry had started in previous ages, along with religious animal sacrifice, the Age of Pisces depicts a magnitude of exploitation never before witnessed in Earth's history. Until modern times, the slaughter of animals generally occurred in a haphazard and unregulated manner in diverse places. The slaughter was then in the open air or undercover, such as at wet markets.

As Fitzgerald (2010) explains, "The first [of three major periods of the development of slaughterhouses] began with increasing concerns about animal slaughtering in the eighteenth century and resulted in 'public slaughterhouse' reforms, which marked the beginning of the concentration of animal slaughter and its movement away from the gaze of the public. Second, slaughterhouses became industrialized, as exemplified by the development of the notorious Union Stockyard in Chicago during the late nineteenth century." These reforms meant that people became physically and psychologically separated from the animals that they consume. In previous eras, animals used to be domesticated to provide meat. This meant constant contact between animals and humans was common, which may indicate a cold trait in the latter. With the advent of slaughterhouses in the post-domestic era, systematic carnage escalated to mass production. One negative aspect of Pisces is that it is prone to addiction, secrecy, and confinement, which may implicitly be associated with the existence of modern-day slaughterhouses.

### Estimated Number of Land Animals Killed for Meat in 2018*

| Animal | Number Killed |
| --- | --- |
| Chickens | 69 billion |
| Pigs | 1.5 billion |
| Turkeys | 656 million |
| Sheep | 574 million |
| Goats | 479 million goats |
| Cattle | 302 million |

*Ritchie, Rosado, and Roser (2017) based on data from the Food and Agriculture Organization of the United Nations (FAO website). The data does not include aquatic animals, eggs, experimented animals, skins, or discarded chicks.

Pisces governs hidden and unpopular subjects, such as marginalized groups, slaughterhouses, and fantasies. The main characteristic of Pisces is self-seclusion in its own parallel world. These traits lead to an era of an anesthetized society that covers up unconscious guilt. As denial is a blatant Piscean trait, most humans deny the origins of meat and are reluctant to discuss such topics.

Pisces governs illusion and escapism, which are present in religious sects and present in the forms of alluring arts, as seen during the Renaissance. Additionally, Pisces granted the spread of theater, music, and novels, besides the use of narcotics as a method of escapism or access to different states of consciousness. Film and television may be considered an interweaving between the fantasizing and creative Pisces and the electric and universalist Aquarius. Paradoxical to the holy wars against nations and individuals, charitable acts also blossomed for the first time among groups and entities, including those promoted by the Roman church. Thus, compassion within religious groups is also a point to note in the Age of Pisces. Schools, convents, religious seclusion, and hospitals are, likewise, notable products of this age.

### Prophesy on the Coming of the Age of Aquarius

As the transition from one age to another develops, it is proposed that in the Gospel of Luke 22:10, Jesus referred to the Age of Aquarius when replying to the apostles asking where they should prepare to celebrate the Passover, the holiday that commemorates the freedom of the Israelites from the Egyptians. He replied, "As you enter the city, a man carrying a jar of water will meet you. Follow him to the house that he enters." The Age of Aquarius is not in the Bible, but studies suggest a correlation between prophetic periods and astrological eras that indicate a spiritual transition in the third millennium CE.

The Second Epistle of Peter states: "Dear friends, do not overlook this one fact: With the Lord, one day is like a thousand years and a thousand years like one day." Knowing that the week has seven days and that the seventh day is the "Shabbat," this verse may hint that

God's week consists of seven thousand years, while His Shabbat lasts for one thousand years.

Within the biblical framework and chronology, the dominant date for the creation of the world was approximately 4000 BCE, and the modern-day Hebrew calendar has since the fourth century CE dated the creation to 3761 BCE. This means that Jesus was born 3761 years after the creation of the world. For a random comparison, the Gregorian calendar of 2030 CE converts to the year 5791 in the Hebrew calendar, which reflects the years since creation in the Book of Genesis.

The Hebrew year 6000 marks the latest time for initiation of the Messianic Age, a time of universal peace, according to classical Jewish sources. Per the Talmud, Midrash, and Zohar, the "due date" for the Messiah's appearance is 6000 years from creation.

In the book of Exodus 20:8–10, the fourth commandment states that "six days you shall labor and do all your work" and the seventh day (the Sabbath) "must be kept holy."

If six days correspond to six millennia and the seventh corresponds to the Messianic Age (6000–7000 Hebrew years), the Messianic age will start in approximately 2240 CE (Matt 1995).

The Gospel of Matthew 20:16 "The last shall be first and the first last" may also suggest that the individuals living on Earth at the last part of creation (before the seventh millennia), will be the first ones to experience the new era.

The transition between astrological ages is gradual, like the changing of seasons. It may start years before its calculated start date and end through the gradual loss of its characteristics as the new age takes over. Orr (2002) and Howell (2013) explain that a transition between ages is denoted by a change of 1 degree (72 years) in the 30 degrees that comprise a constellation. The start of the Age of Aquarius is estimated to be 2150, but its strong influence on world affairs and society is expected to start in the 2070s. The cusp period, during which the transition occurs, is usually 2 to 4 degrees, meaning Aquarian features may have been seen since the 2000s

## Age of Aquarius: 2150 to 4300 CE

Perhaps the first indication that the Age of Aquarius was imminent was the discovery of Aquarius's modern ruling planet, Uranus, in 1781 (Jegatheesan 2013).

In classical Greek mythology, Uranus is the personification of the sky and ruler of the universe. As such, Aquarius universalizes all affairs, as it rules the sky and hence all other constellations. According to Littmann (2004, 10–11), the planet was named after the ancient Greek sky god by Johann Bode.

Uranus, the planet of sudden change, governs astrological areas such as scientific innovation, eccentricity, democratic uprisings, and liberation. It also has influence over electricity, technology, and the internet. In terms of societal impact, Uranus represents radical ideas, rebellion against outdated norms, and a universal connection found in humanitarian groups. Uranus also reveals a cold and analytical nature, as it is the coldest planet in the solar system (Wilkinson 2016).

Uranus's unique features, such as its 98-degree tilt axis causing alternating hemispheres and clockwise rotation, distinguish it as an insurgent planet in astrology. Uranus's discovery, during the era of romanticism, highlights its association with freedom of creative expression.

Aquarius is traditionally ruled by Saturn, a planet commonly characterized by structure and responsibility. Contemporaneously, Aquarius is ruled by Uranus, a planet associated with sudden change and freedom. Combined, the two planets paint the Age of Aquarius in the hues of the responsibility to change and of a sudden change of structure (Woolfolk 2012). Thus, what is understood as the traditional norm may collapse, and humanity must change in order to obtain freedom.

Coinciding with the discovery of Uranus, the Industrial Revolution bolstered a transformation that the world had never witnessed before. This was a technological period of development that radically remodeled rural and agrarian societies in the Old and New Worlds into industrialized and urbanized regions.

Rebellious movements also occurred, such as the independence of the United States in 1776. The event involved Aquarian dimensions of freedom and universalism, and influenced the rest of the colonies in the Americas to pursue their own independence. The French Revolution (1787–1799) occurred soon after. This was a period of great social upheaval in France, aiming to fundamentally alter the relationship between rulers and those they ruled over, as well as to reshape the essence of political authority. The influence of the French Revolution helped to remodel and renew the European and the New World's political establishments. Other triggers and hints of the Age of Aquarius include the discovery and studies of electricity and its properties, telephones, aviation, modern democracy, space exploration, satellites, computers, and genetics.

As a result, it can be posited that cultural aspects will increasingly converge into universal trends rather than local tendencies, reflecting Aquarius's technological interconnectivity and universalistic ideals.

Above all, the Age of Aquarius aims to be constructed on the universalism of knowledge, technology, and freedom, and rejects that which is considered old-fashioned or archaic. The "belief" of Pisces will thus be defeated by the "knowledge" of Aquarius.

Aquarius is represented by air, which represents rationality and intellect, and as a result, this age is expected to disseminate information widely. Hence, control is likely to endure in the hands of each individual as opposed to those of absolute leaders, religious organizations, or monopolist companies.

If in the eras of Taurus, Aries, and Pisces, respectively, the calf, the lamb, and the fish were the symbols in the form of an animal, in the Age of Aquarius the symbol becomes the human. However, this is not meant to extol the human species, but to bring egalitarian status among people. The equality and equity of Aquarius unequivocally extends to all genders, races, and species on the planet.

Aquarius is identified with the Greek myth of the beautiful Ganymede, a young man who was the most beautiful human on Earth. Mesmerized by his beauty, Zeus captured the youth so he could be the cup-bearer of the gods on Olympus. Such symbolism may suggest the ascension of beautiful (benevolent) humans to the highest realms.

In most Indian religions, *samsara* is the "beginning-less" cycle of birth, existence, and death. Samsara is suffering, and suffering is per-petuated by desire and ignorance, resulting in karma.

*Nirvana* is the ultimate spiritual goal, and it marks the release from rebirths in samsara (Buswell and Lopez 2013). In the Buddhist tradition, nirvana has commonly been interpreted as the extinction of the "three poisons" (Keown 2003). Following these lines, it may be tacitly propitious to pair the "three poisons" with zodiac signs commonly associated with such characters: Taurus (greed), Aries (aversion), and Pisces (ignorance), where nirvana is achieved in Aquarius. That said, this concept is a theory established on coincidence, as opposed to a pragmatic ancient teaching.

Aquarius rules the etheric fluids, which are often depicted as the water pouring from a jar. More important than pouring the water is Aquarius's condition as the water bearer, which means that Aquarius holds and distributes the ether of life. Aquarius wields cosmic fluids with such deftness, albeit kindly and equally pouring them to others.

The Age of Pisces has been characterized by the influence of Virgo, a constellation that represents areas such as labor and wages, laws, human rights, and healthcare facilities. Similarly, the Age of Aquarius is thought to have Leo-like qualities. An example of the negative impact of the com-bination of Aquarius and Leo, when in their negative aspects, was seen in the Nazi regime, which harnessed Aquarius's inclinations for changing society combined with Leo's arrogance to achieve political power.

Another destructive example of Aquarius motivated by Leo was the invention of the atomic bomb. Einstein's Aquarian $E = mc^2$ equation met Robert Oppenheimer's Leonine direction of a laboratory, where the latter designed the first atomic bombs (Hewlett and Anderson 1962). In August 1945, these weapons were used in the bombings of Hiroshima and Nagasaki. However, it must also be emphasized that, despite being an Aquarius-Leo aspect, these two occurrences happened during a period where humanity was still morally underdeveloped.

In a spiritually restored world, the submissive line of Pisces, where men are superior to women, one race is superior to another, and humans are superior to animals, will cease to exist. Aquarius will rebel against self-centeredness and selfishness. Not because Aquarius is a better constellation compared to Pisces, but because Aquarius desires the new, eliminating everything that sounds like the status quo of the previous era. Moreover, mysterious dogmas will have few adherents, losing all their manipulative power.

## What Will Happen to Incompatible Spirits in the Age of Aquarius?

From the spiritualist perspective, it is important to remember that the Age of Aquarius will be defined by the emptying of the dense astral regions, since the majority of spirits whose evolutionary levels are not compatible with those of the new Earth will no longer be able to be reincarnated on this planet. Hence, these spirits of "degrading" personalities are to continue their evolutionary journey on another orb, aligned with their current realities.

Dense astral regions, also known as "lower zones," are one of the dimensions of reality created by the reflection of distorted minds of disembodied spirits.

These regions are commonly darkened, grotesque, and insalubrious. There are different lower zones, some of which may be abysmally cruel, where sinister sorcerers and Draconian spirits rule by fear and terror. Others may be seen as similar to the Judeo-Christian purgatory. Such a perception depends on what the minds of the spirits dwelling there create.

Usually, when incarnated spirits have a malignant and vicious nature, which culminates in the agglomeration of antimatter on their souls, they are attracted to these astral regions upon physical death. Following the purging of destructive emotions, those spirits feel "lighter"—therefore, they are able to leave such obscure dimensions and progress to higher dimensions for treatment, charitable work, and reincarnation. Nonetheless, many remain where they are, engulfed in remorse or in ideas of vengeance against those whom they believe caused their "misfortunes" during their physical lives.

Aquarius universalizes metaphysical knowledge with science and vice versa. Therefore, the emotional and spiritual causes of diseases are to be holistically accepted as official medical reports, connecting advanced genetics (an Aquarian branch of biology) with metaphysical factors.

Leo and its warmth brought the Ice Age to an end, while Cancer nourished the regions and led humans to fertile places. Gemini disseminated communication and trade, while Taurus crystallized the first civilizations. Aries reorganized the world through authority and war, affirming the planet as a locale of atonement, while Pisces delivered spirituality and belief, despite the suffering and manipulation of the masses.

As may be noted, every age that emerged during the recent history of humankind has come to give the previous age a continuation, each experiencing the same cycle reflected in a different constellation. However, the next Age of Aquarius is supposed to be different from the last entire cycle of 25,920 years. As described by fig. 8.4, humanity will depart from the previous group of primitive, preparatory, and atoning eras to enter a group of mental, technological, and regenerating ones.

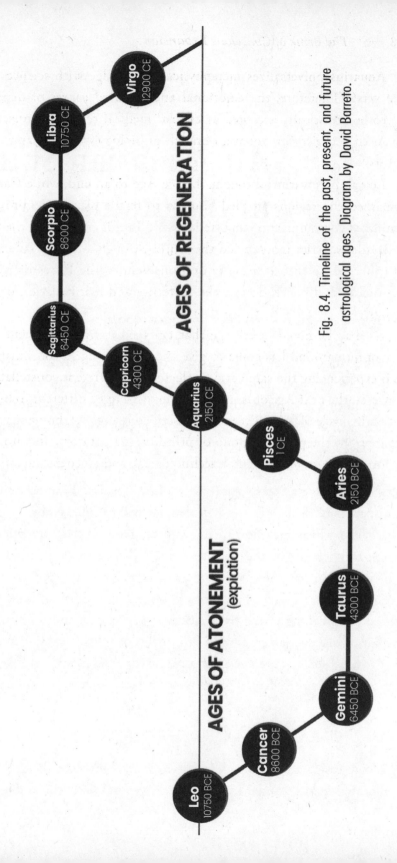

Fig. 8.4. Timeline of the past, present, and future astrological ages. Diagram by David Barreto.

# 9 An Aquarian Shift in the Status Quo

The Age of Aquarius should not be understood as a better period—as though Aquarius was an exceptionally positive sign compared to all others. What allows the Age of Aquarius to be the most favorable age so far is the current spiritual state of the spirits who populate the Earth. Pisces is not to be blamed, just as Aquarius is not to be congratulated, as the qualities of each era only reflect the population's current level of inner peace and altruism.

The condition of the spirits who populate the planet reveals how virtuous or miserable an astrological age will be. That is, if humans evolve altruistic habits, the best qualities of that age will be supplied by the constellation in which they find themselves. Similarly, if the population is corrupt and destructive, the worst features of the astrological period will be presented. In these terms, as humans navigate a transformative shift in consciousness, the Age of Aquarius holds the promise of unlocking its greatest potential, reflecting the collective spirit of humanity. Thus, the dawning of an Aquarian era as well as the influx of enlightened spirits from other celestial spheres, as some anticipate, are expected to mark the Age of Aquarius with unprecedented progress and expansion of consciousness.

## UNDERSTANDING THE STATUS QUO

When the fundamental purpose of a work is to advocate for the spirits allocated in the animal kingdom, it is a moral and ethical duty to reiterate that a world of atonement can only progress to a world of regeneration when the noble and altruistic principles of equality are present between humans and animals.

Regarding animals, the status quo is involves the dolorous routine humans impose on other species. Because of this pain, the status quo must, as a prerequisite in the face of a new era, be reconstructed.

As souls, maltreated beings involuntarily contribute to maintaining the planet's vibrational frequency at sunken levels. Most humans arm themselves with excuses for the carnage that animals endure. The justification for the continuation of animal slaughter fluctuates between the misunderstood diets of pre-*Homo sapiens,* regional culture, and the occasional misinterpretation of religious scriptures.

The uncertainty about the cause for the deficit of peace in the world is typically accompanied by the financing of the butchery of sentient beings, which is insulting to any divine or spiritual law, regardless of religion.

Wars, heinous crimes, extortion, slander, and slavery of workers are unquestionably direct contributors to the paradigm of planet Earth remaining below salutary frequencies. The perpetuation of the existing social structure and values, which includes the slaughter of animals, is also a harmful component, which curtails the planet's ability to advance both morally and technologically.

Despite global hopes for harmony, peace, and happiness, according to the Food and Agriculture Organization of the United Nations (2017), humans cruelly execute approximately 215 million land animals every single day (and that excludes the 4.9 billion fish and other aquatic animals captured daily, according to a 2011 report by the same organization). Each day, more land animals are killed for their meat than people died in wars, massacres, genocide, and urban violence since the start of World War I. That is, from 1914 to 2021, as estimated by Pinto et al. (2014), the 186 million human deaths are, still, fewer in number compared to the amount of land animals killed daily.

The terrestrial psychosphere, which can be understood as the Earth's aura, and generated by thoughts and feelings, is severely affected by the number of animal deaths. Although countless doctrines claim that the Earth's psychosphere is continuously damaged by human-on-human crimes, resentment, and mundane deviations, such theories often neglect the impact of such colossal figures of animal slaughter—which, as previously described, exceeds 5 billion deaths daily.

The term *psychosphere* refers to the spiritual environment of all living beings—especially sentient beings, not just human beings. Thus, planet Earth can only progress to a reality of relative peace and spiritual regeneration once the world's leading cause of suffering ends.

## CHANGING THE STATUS QUO

In the Age of Aquarius, food based on flesh or food obtained through exploitation will be seen as barbaric. Moreover, animal-based food will cease to exist even before the height of the Age of Aquarius, and technologies, as well as the discovery of highly nutritious foods like algae, will be the greatest substitutes for that kind of archaic idea of food. Thus, the change in thinking will bring an end to mass imprisonment, which will include the end of animal slaughterhouses.

The systematization of world conventions will also ban the production and sale of meat, as well as other foods obtained through animal exploitation. However, the movement of change will be initiated by the masses themselves, who will wake up from Piscean torpidity in the face of the attentive Aquarian influence.

Racism, sexism, and social prejudices will also be seen as morally and spiritually immature, emblematic of an embarrassing history.

Overall, Aquarius advances to shift the paradigm and the status quo in a revolution that will amend the imbalances and animosity among humans and between humanity and animals.

### Change Does Not Happen Overnight
The shift in the "collective conscious" refers to a new era about to begin. However, change does not occur overnight, but gradually. Change starts when the frequency of the collective conscious rises in vibration, thereby

resonating with new restoring frequencies from higher dimensions.

As the Earth finds itself in a different reality of consciousness, the individuals and collectives who refrain from adapting to the new way of thinking will be distressed by the astounding new tendencies that begin to replace the old ones. Natural disasters like fires that devastate entire regions, viruses that affect populations worldwide, and wars that cause modern-era exoduses, serve among other reasons to induce humanity to a shift of mental frequencies, thereby substantially changing paradigms. These events do not occur as punishment on stagnant consciousnesses that abstain from progressing, but as a means of eliciting the collective conscious to adapt to different behaviors through affliction, since spiritual evolution via charity and compassion continually fails for most of those who are incarnated in this planet.

This "push" serves as a guarantee that the new frequencies that the planet Earth finds itself in will be compatible with its inhabiting societies. It is worth emphasizing that natural catastrophes, global epidemics, and wars are the materialization of all that is already occurring to those individuals on an ethereal dimension. In other words, physical materialization of calamities are condensed circumstances of that which is already a nonphysical reality, and they are neither created by God nor are they the result of divine punishment. Rather they are collective karma generated by the collective conscious itself.

In the early decades of the twenty-first century, a multitudinous number of consciousnesses from neighboring celestial spheres are to migrate to planet Earth, in furtherance of incarnating amid locals. Such movement of new spirits to planet Earth contributes to the propelling of altruistic behavior, benevolent ideals, and the modernization of societies of all nations.

Comparable migrations have occurred in the past, most notoriously the one that started in the previous Age of Gemini. In those times, spirits native to the Auriga constellation migrated to the planet Earth (Xavier 1939a) and, after millennia of polishing their spiritual imperfections, they have, for the most part, gone back to their homeland. Nevertheless, their presence on Earth proved essential for the development of technology and a further impulse for science, moral values, and the successful perpetuation of humankind.

According to Divaldo Franco (2020), spirits from Eta Tauri, a star in the northwest of the Taurus constellation, are gradually permeating the Earth's families and cultures, bringing the essence of altruism to Earth. At an equal pace, earthly spirits identified with animosity, abominable cruelty, and those prone to heinous criminality are repeatedly denied reincarnation in the terrestrial sphere.

Conjointly, the average human is welcome to continue their evolution on Earth, evolving through the practice of universal compassion, charity, and by virtue of learning via study. There is no such divine arrangement that refuses certain spirits from reincarnating on Earth. For some, their own spiritual frequency will naturally fail to adapt to a world where most inhabitants create a sympathetic and restorative collective conscious.

### Veganism as Norm

Considering the proposition of a paradigm shift, veganism emerges as one of the fundamentals of a new, egalitarian, and morally progressive era. Veganism is the principle and style of living that suggests the abstention from exploitation, abuse, and profiteering of animals for food, entertainment, clothing, sports, and laboratory tests.

The adoption of veganism, which will prove to be a firm tendency as opposed to a trend, aligns with the frequencies of the Age of Aquarius, which implores equality and universalism of rights, leaving behind all customs that are archaic and unjust. Nevertheless, veganism is still considered taboo among various spiritualists and proponents of the "new era," as the subject is often interpreted as "nonesoteric," or an agenda promoted by vegan militants. Still, a small number of spiritualists are attempting to promote the concept, albeit detached from the labels.

Veganism is still taboo in general spiritualistic and esoteric circles. To begin to break that taboo, the history of human slavery may convey an example of how the turpitudes of society, stationed in denial and egoistical reasoning, are capable of supporting an abominable system throughout millennia. In terms of slavery in Greece, Egypt, sub-Saharan Africa, Europe, and the Americas, argumentation to per-petuate such practice at one time included philosophical, religious, and political statements such as, "It's natural that some people are slaves" (White 2012); "Slaves are inferior beings" (Taylor 2016); "Slavery is good for slaves" (De Wet 2016); "Some individuals are naturally slaves, hence they need to be ruled" (Goodey 1999); "Slavery would be rather difficult to abolish" (Goodey 1999); "Slaves are essential to certain industries" (Hampton 2015, 25); "Slavery is legal" (Ingersoll 2015, 205); "Slavery is supported by the Bible" (Ingersoll 2015); "Slavery is accept-able in this culture" (Rushdoony 1973, 137); "Living in slavery is better than starving to death" (Aristotle). Today, these statements are seen as deplorable. Society will see the rationale for eating meat as such in the future.

Not only is the spreading of veganism essential, but also the intro-duction of practices that are less harmful to the environment, such as the reduction in consumption of pernicious materials, solar and wind power, and even the production of electricity from the air. The climate crisis is also triggering a greater interest in self-sustainable vehicles and the replacement of various equipment by alternatives less degrading to the planet.

The new winds are to deliver the regenerated Earth with wireless electricity, synthetic antibodies, easily modified genes, practically non-invasive surgeries made by refined lasers, widespread artificial intel-ligence, and the recycling of materials into environmentally friendly alternatives, such as biodegradable goods. The latter will decrease the extraction of natural resources to nearly zero. The replanting of defor-ested areas and the cleansing of the oceans and soil will also generate many jobs and renew the Earth.

Although the winds of change are likely to be experienced before the calculated years of the new age, they will not be fully experienced before veganism becomes the norm. A plant-based diet is the single big-gest step one can take to reduce their environmental impact (Poore and Nemecek 2018), which invariably generates collective karma. It is criti-cal to emphasize that the impact of animal agriculture on the planet is the most serious ecological and moral form of terrorism and subjugation of animals, the land, and, ultimately, humans.

As long as exploitative industries are financed by humans, the planet Earth cannot enter into a completely restored reality, and that includes the locales in the astral dimensions closer to the Earth.

If one individual can abstain from consuming products that come from animal cruelty, and is therefore not affected by harmful energy, the same concept can be applied to the entire world.

Veganism has never had such a presence on the face of the Earth before. Neither in Egypt, nor in Sumer, nor in China, nor in India. Therefore, it is a thrilling moment to experience the rise of a movement trying to finally substitute and rebel against the primitive status quo that holds the planet from evolving to a new era of universal compassion, equality, and moral progress.

The vegan movement appears to be humanity's best chance to break the cycle of violence against animals detailed in in this book, including the atrocities caused for their flesh, the hypocritical use of their symbolism, and sacrifices within many religious cults.

Veganism relates to the principles of equality and respect for every species, emphasizing their right to exist in freedom. Regardless of labels and nomenclatures, the principles of veganism are some of the most spiritual, sincere, and honorable qualities one can hold. Ultimately, "spirituality" means being concerned with the spirit and its affairs, as opposed to the material world or physical surroundings. Thus, veganism offers the least paradoxical conduct for those claiming to be on the right side, and furthers the advancement of the planet Earth toward a change in thinking at a spiritual level.

# Recommended Reading

Banerjee, K., and P. Bloom. 2013. "Would Tarzan Believe in God? Conditions for the Emergence of Religious Belief." *Trends in Cognitive Sciences* 17, no. 1: 7–8.

Barkow, J., L. Cosmides, and J. Tooby, eds. 1992. *The Adapted Mind: Evolutionary Psychology and the Generation of Culture.* New York: Oxford University Press.

Besant, Annie, and W. Charles Leadbeater. 1901. *Thought-Forms.* London: Theosophical Publishing Society.

Borges, Wagner. 2005. *Extraphysical and Projective Teachings (by Sanat Khum Maat).* Originally published in Portuguese in São Paulo by Madras. English version available online at the Instituto de Pesquisas Projeciológicas e Bioenergéticas website and on Scribd.

Boyer, Pascal. 1994. *The Naturalness of Religious Ideas: A Cognitive Theory of Religion.* Berkeley: University of California Press.

Boyer, Pascal. 2003. "Religious Thought and Behaviour as By-products of Brain Function." *Trends in Cognitive Sciences* 7, no. 3: 119–24.

Grant, C. 2006. *The No-Nonsense Guide to Animal Rights.* Oxford: New Internationalist.

Guthrie, S. 1995. *Faces in the Clouds: A New Theory of Religion.* Oxford University Press.

Henrich, J., and R. McElreath. 2007. "Dual Inheritance Theory: The Evolution of Human Cultural Capacities and Cultural Evolution." In *Oxford Handbook of Evolutionary Psychology,* edited by R. Dunbar & L. Barrett, 555–70. Oxford University Press.

Hodge, K. M. 2008. "Descartes' Mistake: How Afterlife Beliefs Challenge the Assumption That Humans Are Intuitive Cartesian Substance Dualists." *Journal of Cognition and Culture* 8, no. 3, 387–415.

Houston, Stephen D. 2004. *The First Writing: Script Invention as History and Process*. Cambridge: Cambridge University Press.

Järnefelt, E., C. F. Canfield, and D. Kelemen. 2015. "The Divided Mind of a Disbeliever: Intuitive Beliefs about Nature as Purposefully Created among Different Groups of Non-religious Adults." *Cognition* 140: 72–88.

Jong, J., J. Halberstadt, and M. Bluemke. 2012. "Foxhole Atheism, Revisited: The Effects of Mortality Salience on Explicit and Implicit Religious Belief." *Journal of Experimental Social Psychology* 48, no. 5:983–89.

Kemmerer, Lisa. 2012. *Animals and World Religions*. Oxford University Press.

Kozłowski, Stefan Karol. 1999. *The Eastern Wing of the Fertile Crescent: Late Prehistory of Greater Mesopotamian Lithic Industries*. Oxford: Archaeopress, 1999.

McCauley, R. N., and E. T. Lawson. 2002. *Bringing Ritual to Mind: Psychological Foundations of Cultural Forms*. Cambridge, UK: Cambridge University Press.

Norris, P., and R. Inglehart. 2012. *Sacred and Secular: Religion and Politics Worldwide*. 2nd ed. Cambridge: Cambridge University Press.

Padmanabh, S., 1998. *The Jaina Path of Purification*. Delhi: Motilal Banarsidass.

Parker, D., and J. Parker. 2009. *Parkers' Encyclopedia of Astrology*. London: Watkins Publishing.

Pathak S. 2013. *Figuring Religions: Comparing Ideas, Images and Activities*. Albany: University of New York Press.

Penrose, Roger. 2016. *Fashion, Faith, and Fantasy in the New Physics of the Universe*. Princeton, N.J.: Princeton University Press.

Purzycki, B. G., and A. K. Willard. 2016. "MCI Theory: A Critical Discussion." *Religion, Brain & Behavior* 6, no. 3: 207–48.

Slone, D. J. 2004. *Theological Incorrectness: Why Religious People Believe What They Shouldn't*. Oxford University Press.

Story, Francis. 1964. *The Place of Animals in Buddhism*. Buddhist Publication Society.

White, C. 2016. "The Cognitive Foundations of Reincarnation." *Method & Theory in the Study of Religion* 28, no. 3.

Wilson, D. S. 2003. *Darwin's Cathedral: Evolution, Religion, and the Nature of Society*. Chicago: University Of Chicago Press.

# References

Adler, J. 1999. "Response to Rodney Taylor, 'Of Animals and Man: The Confucian Perspective.'" Presented at the Conference on Religion and Animals. Cambridge: Harvard–Yenching Institute (May 21).

Ahlfort, K. 2011. "Genetic Study Confirms: First Dogs Came from East Asia." Royal Institute of Technology news release. Uppsala University.

Allen, John Romilly. 1884. *Notes on Early Christian Symbolism*. Society of Antiquaries of Scotland.

Andersen, B., and Borns, H. 1997. *The Ice Age World: An Introduction to Quaternary History and Research with Emphasis on North America and Northern Europe During the Last 2.5 Million Years*. Oslo: Universitetsforlaget.

Anderson, E. N., and L. Raphals. 2007. "Daoism and Animals." In *A Communion of Subjects: Animals in Religion, Science, and Ethics,* edited by Paul Waldau and Kimberly Patton, 275–90. New York: Columbia University Press.

Andrade, Edward Neville da Costa. 1959. "Doppler and the Doppler Effect." *Endeavour:* 14–19.

Aristotle. 1985. In *The Politics,* translated by C. Lord. Chicago: University of Chicago Press.

Arroyo, Stephen. 1978. *Astrology, Karma and Transformation: The Inner Dimensions of the Birth Chart*. Davis, Calif.: CRCS Publications.

Ashcroft, F. 2002. *Life at the Extremes: The Science of Survival*. Berkeley: University of California Press.

Baconnier, S., and S. B. Lang. 2004. "Calcite Microcrystals in the Pineal Gland of the Human Brain: Second Harmonic Generators and Possible Piezoelectric Transducers." *IEEE Transactions on Dielectrics and Electrical Insulation* 11, no. 2 (April): 203–9.

Baggott, Jim. 2012. *Higgs: The Invention and Discovery of the 'God Particle.'* Oxford: Oxford University Press.

Baird, Christopher S. 2013. "How Does the Expansion of the Universe Make Outer Space a Vacuum?" Science Questions with Surprising Answers website (October 8).

Baldwin, J. A. 1975. "Notes and Speculations on the Domestication of the Cat in Egypt." *Anthropos. Nomos Verlagsgesellschaft,* 428–48.

Balkwill, Richard. 1994. *Food and Feasts in Ancient Egypt.* New Discovery.

Balmurli, N., and J. Suraj. 2018. "'Provincialising' Vegetarianism Putting Indian Food Habits in Their Place." *Economic and Political Weekly* 53, no. 9.

Barbault, Andre. 2016. *Planetary Cycles: Mundane Astrology.* Astrological Association.

Barreto, D. 2019. *The Supernatural Science: Theory and Magic.* London.

Barton, J. 1998. *The Cambridge Companion to Biblical Interpretation.* Cambridge: Cambridge University Press.

Basheer, Radhika, et al. 2012. "Control of Sleep and Wakefulness." *Physiological Reviews* 92, no. 3 (July): 1087–187.

BBC. 2016. "Yulin Dog Meat Festival Begins in China amid Widespread Criticism." BBC online. (June 21).

Bellwood, P. 2004. *First Farmers: The Origins of Agricultural Societies.* Wiley–Blackwell.

Benedeti, Marcel. 2012. *All Animals Go to Heaven.* Spiritual Light Publishing.

Berresford, P. (1998) 2003. *The Ancient World of the Celts.* London: Robinson Publishing.

Berridge K. C., and T. E. Robinson. 2016. "Liking, Wanting, and the Incentive-Sensitization Theory of Addiction." *Am Psychol* 71, no. 8 (Nov): 670–79.

Best, Shivali. 2019. "China's Shang Dynasty Buried Puppies Alive, Archaeologists Reveal." Daily Mirror online (May 8).

Beyssade, J-M. 1992. *The Idea of God and Proofs of His Existence in The Cambridge Companion to Descartes.* Cambridge: Cambridge University Press.

Bird, R., Warren E. Stewart, and Edwin N. Lightfoot. 2007. *Transport Phenomena.* 2nd ed. Hoboken, N.J.: John Wiley & Sons.

Blakeley, Donald. 2003. "Listening to the Animals: The Confucian View of Animal Welfare." *Journal of Chinese Philosophy* 30, no. 2 (May 6): 137–57.

Blavatsky, H. P. 1889. *The Key to Theosophy.* London: Theosophical Publishing Company.

Bocking, B. 1997. *A Popular Dictionary of Shinto.* Rev. ed. Richmond: Curzon.

Borchert, Donald M., ed. 2006. *Encyclopedia of Philosophy.* 9 vol. set, 2nd ed. New York: Macmillan Reference.

Borsboom, Wim. 2000. "The Major Chakras and Their Petals." Available online.

Brazier, Yvette. 2019. "What Are Bacteria and What Do They Do?" MedicalNewsToday website (February 12).

Breen, John, and Mark Teeuwen. 2010. *A New History of Shinto.* Chichester: Wiley–Blackwell.

Brown, F., et al. (1849) 1991 reprint. *The Brown-Driver-Briggs Hebrew and English Lexicon.* Carol Stream, Ill.: Hendrickson.

Brown, R. 1991. *Ganesh: Studies of an Asian God.* Albany: State University of New York.

Bruno, Thomas, et al. 2005. *CRC Handbook of Fundamental Spectroscopic Correlation Charts.* Boca Raton, Fla.: CRC Press.

Burke–Gaffney, W. 1937. "Kepler and the Star of Bethlehem." *Journal of the Royal Astronomical Society of Canada* 31:417.

Burkert, W. 1983. *Homo Necans: The Anthropology of Ancient Greek Sacrificial Ritual and Myth.* Translated by P. Bing. Berkeley: Univ. of California Press.

Burton, A. 1973. *Diodorus Siculus.* Book 1: A Commentary. Leiden: Brill.

Buswell, Robert E., Jr., and Donald S. Lopez Jr. 2013. *The Princeton Dictionary of Buddhism.* Princeton, N.J.: Princeton University Press.

Chang, Kwang-chih. 1976. *Early Chinese Civilization: Anthropological Perspectives.* Cambridge: Harvard University Press.

Chang, K. C. 1977. *Food in Chinese Culture: Anthropological and Historical Perspectives.* New Haven, Conn.: Yale University Press.

Chen, Y. 2012. *Confucionismo como religião: controvérsias e consequências.* Leiden: Brill.

Cline, Eric H., and Jill Rubalcaba. 2004. *The World in Ancient Times: The Ancient Egyptian World.* Oxford: Oxford University Press.

Coogan, M. 2009. *A Brief Introduction to the Old Testament.* Oxford: Oxford University Press.

De Bary, William Theodore, and Irene Bloom. 1999. *Sources of Chinese Tradition.* New York: Columbia University Press.

Demand, Nancy. 1996. *A History of Ancient Greece.* New York: McGraw-Hill.

Denisenko V.N., and Y. X. Zheng. 2021. "Twelve Chinese Zoosigns of Zodiak: Tradition and Modernity." *RUDN Journal of Language Studies Semiotics and Semantics* 12, no. 4: 1299–313.

Department of Animal Husbandry & Dairying. 2019. *Dairying and Fisheries.* India: Ministry of Agriculture & Farmers' Welfare. Annual Report 2018–19. Accessed online July 30, 2020.

De Vries, A. 1976. *Dictionary of Symbols and Imagery.* Amsterdam: North–Holland Publishing.

De Wet, C. L. 2016. "The Punishment of Slaves in Early Christianity: The Views of Some Selected Church Fathers." *Acta Theologica* 23, no. 1: 263.

Dirac, P. 1965. *Physics Nobel Lectures 1922–1941.* Amsterdam–London–New York: Elsevier.

Dittrich, W., and H. Gies. 2000. *Probing the Quantum Vacuum: Perturbative Effective Action Approach in Quantum Electrodynamics and Its Application.* Berlin: Springer.

Eberhard, Wolfram. 1941. *A History of China.* Alfred Kröner Verlag.

Energy Education Encyclopedia. n.d. Energy Education Encyclopedia website. s.v. "thermal energy."

Eng, Khoo Boo. 2019. *Understanding Chinese Culture in Relation to Tao.* Singapore: Partridge Publishing.

Engels, D. W. 1999. *Classical Cats. The Rise and Fall of the Sacred Cat.* London, New York: Routledge.

Fan, Ruiping. 2010. "How Should We Treat Animals? A Confucian Reflection." *Dao* 9 (January 12): 79–96.

Fingarette, H. 1972. *Confucius: The Secular as Sacred.* New York: Harper.

Fitzgerald, A. J. 2010. "A Social History of the Slaughterhouse: From Inception to Contemporary Implications." *Research in Human Ecology* 17.

Flores, D. 1999. "The Funerary Sacrifice of Animals During the Pre-dynastic Period." Doctoral thesis. The University of Toronto.

Food and Agriculture Organization of the United Nations. 2011. "Fishery and Aquaculture Statistics." FAO website. Accessed September 27, 2019.

———. 2017. "Data of Land Animals Slaughtered." FAOSTAT website. Accessed September 27, 2019.

Foster, John. 1889. "Papers on Indian Reform: Sanitary, Material, Social, Moral and Religious." Christian Vernacular Education Society (original from Oxford University).

Franco, Divaldo. 2020. *On the Way to the World of Regeneration.* Rio de Janeiro: FEB.

French, A. P., and P. J. Kennedy, eds. 1985. *Niels Bohr: A Centenary Volume.* Cambridge, Mass.: Harvard University Press.

Friedmann, A. 1999. "On the Curvature of Space." *General Relativity and Gravitation* 31:1999–2000.

Frothingham, A. L. 1916. "Babylonian Origin of Hermes the Snake-God, and of the Caduceus I." *American Journal of Archaeology* 20, no. 2 (April–June): 175–211.

Fuller, C. 2004. *The Camphor Flame: Popular Hinduism and Society in India.* Princeton, N.J.: Princeton University Press.

Fuller, M. F. 2004. *The Encyclopedia of Farm Animal Nutrition.* Wallingford, U.K.: Centre for Agriculture and Bioscience International.

Furst, Dab. 2011. *Surfing Aquarius: How to Ace the Wave of Change.* San Francisco, Calif.: Weiser Books.

Gauss, C. F. 1801. *The Shaping of Arithmetic After Disquisitiones Arithmeticae.* Latin vers.

Goldenweiser A. 1910. "Totemism: An Analytical Study." *Journal of American Folk-Lore* 23:179–293.

Goodey, C. F. 1999. "Politics, Nature, and Necessity: Were Aristotle's Slaves Feeble Minded?" *Political Theory* 27, no. 2: 203–24.

Goodman, Martin, Jeremy Cohen, and David Sorkin. 2002. *The Oxford Handbook of Jewish Studies.* Oxford: Oxford University Press.

Goswami, Amit. 2011. *The Quantum Doctor: A Quantum Physicist Explains the Healing Power of Integrative Medicine.* Charlottesville, Va.: Hampton Roads.

Gould, J. L. 1984. "Magnetic Field Sensitivity in Animals." *Annual Review of Physiology* 46:585–98.

Green, M. 1992. *Animals in Celtic Life and Myth.* London: Routledge.

———. 2005. *Exploring the World of the Druids.* London: Thames & Hudson.

Greene, Joshua. 2013. *Hanuman: The Heroic Monkey God.* Mumbai: Jaico Publishing.

Greenwald, A. G., M. R. Klinger, and E. S. Schuh. 1995. "Activation by Marginally Perceptible ('Subliminal') Stimuli. Dissociation of Unconscious from Conscious Cognition." *Journal of Experimental Psychology: General* 124, no. 1: 22–42.

Gribbin, J. 2000. *Q is for Quantum. An Encyclopedia of Particle Physics.* New York: Simon & Schuster.

Grimes John. 1996. *A Concise Dictionary of Indian Philosophy: Sanskrit Terms Defined in English.* New York: State University of New York Press, 1996.

Guerin, S., S. A. M. Tofail, and D. Thompson. 2018. "Longitudinal

Piezoelectricity in Natural Calcite Materials: Preliminary Studies." *IEEE Transactions on Dielectrics and Electrical Insulation* 25, no. 3 (June): 803–7.

Haikal, Fayza. n.d. "Ra, the Creator God of Ancient Egypt." American Research Center in Egypt website.

Hampton, G. 2015. *Imagining Slaves and Robots in Literature, Film, and Popular Culture*. Washington, D.C.: Lexington Books.

Hao, Song Zhen. 2011. *Shang Dynasty History: Outline of History in Shang Dynasty* (Chinese edition). China Social Sciences Press.

Harrison, Edward Robert. 2000. *Cosmology: The Science of the Universe*. Cambridge: Cambridge University Press.

Harshananda (Swami). 1987. *Hindu Gods and Goddesses*. Chennai: Sri Ramakrishna Math.

Harvati, K., et al. 2019. "Apidima Cave Fossils Provide Earliest Evidence of *Homo sapiens* in Eurasia." *Nature* 571, no. 7766 (July):500–504.

Harvey, P. 2000. *An Introduction to Buddhist Ethics: Foundations, Values and Issues*. Cambridge: Cambridge University Press.

Hauck, Dennis William. 1999. *The Emerald Tablet: Alchemy of Personal Transformation*. New York: Penguin.

Hawking, Stephen W. 1966. "Properties of Expanding Universes." Doctoral thesis, University of Cambridge, 1966.

Heibron, J. L. 1985. "Bohr's First Theories of the Atom." *Physics Today* 38, no. 10: 28.

Henshilwood, C., and C. Marean. 2003. "The Origin of Modern Human Behavior: Critique of the Models and Their Test Implications." *Current Anthropology* 44, no. 5: 627–51.

Hewlett, R., and O. Anderson. 1962. *The New World, 1939–1946. A History of the United States Atomic Energy Commission*. University Park: Pennsylvania State University Press.

Hodson, Geoffrey. 1952. *The Kingdom of the Gods*. Adyar, India: Theosophical Publishing House.

Hoffner, Harry A. 1997. *The Laws of the Hittites: A Critical Edition*. Brill.

Holler, F. J., D. A. Skoog, and S. R. Crouch. 2007. *Principles of Instrumental Analysis*. 6th ed. Cengage Learning.

Howell, Alice O. 2013. *The Heavens Declare: Astrological Ages and the Evolution of Consciousness*. Wheaton, Ill.: Quest Books.

Hubble, Edwin. 1929. "A Relation between Distance and Radial Velocity among

Extra-Galactic Nebulae." *Proceedings of the National Academy of Sciences* 15 (January 17): 168–73.

Ikram, Salima. 2005. *Divine Creatures: Animal Mummies in Ancient Egypt.* Cairo: American University in Cairo Press.

———. 2015. "Speculations on the Role of Animal Cults in the Economy of Ancient Egypt." In *Apprivoiser Le Sauvage/Taming the Wild,* edited by M. Massiera, B. Mathieu, and F. Rouffet, 211–28. Montpellier: Cahiers de l'Égypte Nilotique et Méditerranéenne.

Ikram, S., Ruhan Slabbert, Izak Cornelius, and Anton Du Plessis. 2015. "Fatal Force–Feeding or Gluttonous Gagging? The Death of Kestrel." *Journal of Archaeological Science* 63:72–77.

Indian Census. 2014. Sample Registration, Religion. National System Baseline Survey. Accessed online September 5, 2019.

Ingersoll, J. 2015. *Building God's Kingdom: Inside the World of Christian Reconstruction.* Oxford University Press.

International Chimpanzee Chromosome 22 Consortium. 2004. "DNA sequence and comparative analysis of chimpanzee chromosome 22." *Nature* 429 (May 27):382–88.

Ishige, Naomichi. 2001. *The History and Culture of Japanese Food.* New York: Columbia University Press.

Iyer, S., and D. Cook, dirs. 2016. *Gods in Shackles.* India–Canada.

Jegatheesan, R. 2013. "Uranus: Discovery of the Seventh Planet in Sun Family, 26th of April, 1781." *Discovery* 4, no. 10: 3–4.

Johnson, Paul Christopher. 2002. *Secrets, Gossip, and Gods: The Transformation of Brazilian Candomblé.* Oxford and New York: Oxford University Press.

Johnson, Scott. 2017. *Why Did Ancient Civilizations Fail?* Routledge.

Joos, G. 1951. *Theoretical Physics.* London–Glasgow: Blackie and Son.

Jung, C. 1960. "Instinct and the Unconscious." *Collected Works.* Vol. 8, *The Structures and Dynamics of the Psyche.* London: Routledge & Kegan Paul Ltd.

———. 1964. *Man and His Symbols.* New York: Anchor Press.

———. 1969. *Collected Works.* Vol. 9, *The Archetypes and Collective Unconscious.* London: Routledge & Kegan Paul Ltd.

Kanev, I., K. A. DeHaai, A. Z. Van Dyke, J. N. Sanmann, and M. M. Hess, et al. 2012 "Are the Structural and Functional Similarity between the Human Chromosomes and the Electrical Transformer Coincidental." Electrostatics Joint Conference, Cambridge, Ontario (Canada), June 12–14.

Kanev, I., et al. 2013. "Searching for Electrical Properties, Phenomena and Mechanisms in the Construction and Function of Chromosomes." *Computational and Structural Biotechnology* 6, no. 7 (June 27).

Kardec, Allan. 1857. *Le Livre des Esprits*. E Dentu: Paris. Translated to English in 2005 under the title *The Spirits' Book*. New York: Cosimo Classics.

Karenga, Maulana. (1994) 2003. *Maat: The Moral Ideal in Ancient Egypt—A Study in Classical African Ethics*. Taylor & Francis.

Katz, Paul. 2008. *Divine Justice: Religion and the Development of Chinese Legal Culture*. Routledge.

Keightley, David. 1989. *Shang Religion: The Classic Phase*. Berkeley: University of California Press.

———. 1990. "Review: Sources of Shang History: Two Major Oracle-Bone Collections Published in the People's Republic of China." *Journal of the American Oriental Society* 110, no. 1 (Jan–Mar): 39–59.

———. 1999. "The Shang: China's First Historical Dynasty." In *The Cambridge History of Ancient China*, edited by M. Loewe and E. Shaughnessy. Cambridge: Cambridge University Press.

Keown, D. 2003. *A Dictionary of Buddhism*. Oxford: Oxford University Press.

Klein, R. 1995. "Anatomy, Behaviour, and Modern Human Origins." *Journal of World Prehistory* 9, no. 2: 167–98.

Koch, C. 2004. *The Quest for Consciousness: A Neurobiological Approach*. Denver, Colo.: Roberts & Co.

Krause, Carl. 1931. "Hostia" *RE* suppl. 5:236–82.

Langdon, S., and A. Gardiner. 1920. "The Treaty of Alliance between Hattusili, King of the Hittites and the Pharaoh Ramesses II of Egypt." *Journal of Egyptian Archaeology* 6, no. 3: 179–205.

Laveesh, B. 2009. *Indian States at a Glance, 2008–2009. Performance, Facts and Figures*. West Bengal: Pearson Education India.

Laynton, Robert. 2013. *Behind the Masks of God*. Stoke-on-Trent: Companion Guides.

Leadbeater, Charles Webster. 1902. *Man, Visible and Invisible*. London: Theosophical Publishing Society.

Leão, Delfim, and Peter Rhodes. 2016. *The Laws of Solon*. London: I.B. Tauris.

Lee, Pole, Joseph Choi, and Ryan Sun. 2020. "Japanese Food and Metaphysics." Emory University blog.

Lemaître, G. (1927 in French) 1931. "A Homogeneous Universe of Constant Mass and Increasing Radius Accounting for the Radial Speed of Extra-galactic Nebulae." Translation published by the *Monthly Notices of the Royal Astronomical Society* 91:483–90. Originally published in French by the Université catholique de Louvain.

Levenda, Peter. 2020. *The Secret Temple: Masons, Mysteries, and the Founding of America.* Lake Worth, Fla.: Nicolas Hays.

Lilly, J. 1987. *Communication between Man and Dolphin: The Possibilities of Talking with Other Species.* New York: Julian Press.

Lilly, John C., and Alice M. Miller. 1961. "Vocal Exchanges between Dolphins." *Science* 134, no. 3493 (December 8).

Lima, S. L., and J. M. O'Keefe. 2013. "Do Predators Influence the Behaviour of Bats?" *Biological Reviews of the Cambridge Philosophical Society* 88, no. 3: 626–44.

Linsley, J., L. Scarsi, P. Spillantini, and Y. Takahashi. 1997. "Space Air Watch: Observation of the Earth Atmosphere from the ISSA Space Station." Proceedings of the 25th International Cosmic Ray Conference. Held July 30–August 6 in Durban, South Africa. Vol. 5. pp. 385.

Lipner, J. 2012. *Hindus: Their Religious Beliefs and Practices.* 2nd ed. London: Routledge.

Lipton, Bruce. 2005. *The Biology of Belief.* London: Hay House.

Littmann, M. 2004. *Planets Beyond: Discovering the Outer Solar System.* Courier Dover Publications.

Liu, Li, and Xingcan Chen. 2012. *The Archaeology of China: From the Late Paleolithic to the Early Bronze Age.* Cambridge: Cambridge University Press.

Lochtefeld, G. 2001. *The Illustrated Encyclopedia of Hinduism.* New York: Rosen Publishing.

Locke, John. 1689. *The Works of John Locke in Nine Volumes.* Vol. 1, *An Essay Concerning Human Understanding. Part 1.* Rivington. Available from the Online Library of Liberty.

Lodish, H., et al. 2000. "Chemical Equilibrium." In *Molecular Cell Biology.* 4th edition. New York: W. H. Freeman.

Lodish, H., A. Berk, and S. L. Zipursky. 2000. "Molecular Cell Biology: Section 21.4." In *Neurotransmitters, Synapses, and Impulse Transmission.* 4th ed. New York: W. H. Freeman.

Loewe, M., and E. Shaughnessy. 1999. *The Cambridge History of Ancient China: From the Origins of Civilization to 221 BCE.* Cambridge: Cambridge University Press.

Loewe, Michael, and Edward L. Shaughnessy. 2008. In *The Shang: China's*

*First Historical Dynasty*, edited by David Keightley. Cambridge: Cambridge University Press.

Maes, Hercílio. 1959. *Physiology of the Soul*. Brazil: Hercílio Maes Institute. Mediumistic work dictated by the spirit Ramatis to the medium Hercílio Maes.

———. 1964. *Elucidations from Beyond*. Brazil: Hercílio Maes Institute. Mediumistic work dictated by the spirit Ramatis to the medium Hercílio Maes.

Martin, Graham. 1982. "An Owl's Eye: Schematic Optics and Visual Performance in *Strix aluco L.*" *Journal of Comparative Physiology* 145: 341–49.

Matt, Daniel C. 1995. *The Essential Kabbalah: The Heart of Jewish Mysticism*. New York: HarperCollins.

McBrearty, S., and A. Brooks. 2000. "The Revolution That Wasn't: A New Interpretation of the Origin of Modern Human Behaviour." *Journal of Human Evolution* 39, no. 5: 453–563.

McGlashen, Andy. 2019. "Here's Why Birds Rub Their Beaks on Stuff." Audubon website (May 1).

McKnight, L. M., J. Adams, A. Chamberlain, S. D. Atherton-Woolham, and R. Bibb. 2015. "Application of Clinical Imaging and 3D Printing to the Identification of Anomalies in an Ancient Egyptian Animal Mummy." *Journal of Archaeological Science* 3:328–32.

Merrill, William L., and Ives Goddard. 2002. *Anthropology, History, and American Indians: Essays in Honor of William Curtis Sturtevant*. Washington, D.C.: Smithsonian Institution Press.

Meyer, Susan. 2016. *The Neolithic Revolution*. Buffalo, N.Y.: Rosen Publishing.

Michaels, A. 2004. *Hinduism: Past and Present*. Princeton, N.J.: Princeton University Press.

Milner, E. 2010. *A Dialogue on Christianity*. iUniverse.

Ministry of Fisheries, Animal Husbandry and Dairying (of India). 2020. "Basic Animal Husbandry & Fisheries Statistics." Animal Husbandry Statistics Division, DADF, GoI website.

Motoyama, Hiroshi. (1981) 1988. *Theory of the Chakras: Bridge to Higher Consciousness*. Wheaton, Ill.: Theosophical Publishing House.

Murray, A. 1986. "Medieval Christmas." *History Today* 36, no. 12: 31–39.

Nelson, J. K. 1996. *A Year in the Life of a Shinto Shrine*. Seattle–London: University of Washington Press.

Nguyen, Trung. 2016. *History of Gods*. N.P.: EnCognitive.

Nidhin T. 2016. "Gods in Shackles Strikes a Tender Chord." *Deccan Chronicle* July 3.

Nijhout, Frederik. 1990. "Problems and Paradigms: Metaphors and the Role of Genes in Development." *BioEssays* 12, no. 9: 441–46.

———. 1991. *The Development and Evolution of Butterfly Wing Patterns.* Singapore: Springer Nature.

Nissen, H., P. Damerow, and R. Englund. 1993. *Archaic Bookkeeping: Early Writing and Techniques of Economic Administration in the Ancient Near East.* Chicago: University of Chicago Press.

Noble, T., et al. 2013. *Western Civilization: Beyond Boundaries.* Boston: Cengage Learning.

Norris, Kenneth S., John H. Prescott, Paul V. Asa-Dorian, and Paul Perkins. 1961. "An Experimental Demonstration of Echolocation Behavior in the Porpoise, *Tursiops truncatus,* (Montagu)." *The Biological Bulletin* 120, no. 2.

Offner, C. B. 1979. "Shinto." In *The World's Religions,* 4th ed., edited by N. Anderson, 191–218. Leicester: Inter–Varsity Press.

O'Hara, A. M., and F. Shanahan. 2006. "The Gut Flora as a Forgotten Organ." *EMBO Reports* 7, no. 7: 688–93.

Orr, Marjorie. 2002. *The Astrological History of the World.* Vega Books.

Pal, B., A. K. Ghosal, A. P. Minj, and R. K. Ghosh. 2013 "Comparative Histomorphological Study of the Pineal Gland in Human and Fowl." *Al Ameen Journal of Medical Science* 6, no. 1: 80–84.

Phelps, N. 2004. *The Great Compassion: Buddhism & Animal Rights.* New York: Lantern Books.

Pinch, Geraldine. 2004. *Egyptian Mythology: A Guide to the Gods, Goddesses, and Traditions of Ancient Egypt.* Oxford: Oxford University Press.

Pinto, C., A. M. Lopes, and J. A. Tenreiro Machado. 2014. "Casualties Distribution in Human and Natural Hazards." In *Mathematical Methods in Engineering,* 173–80. Springer.

Place, R., and R. Guiley. 2009. *Magic and Alchemy.* New York: Chelsea House Publishers.

Poore, J., and T. Nemecek. 2018. "Reducing Food's Environmental Impacts through Producers and Consumers." *Science* 360, no. 6392 (June 1): 987–92.

Powell, Arthur. 1926. *The Astral Body and Other Astral Phenomena.* London: Theosophical Publishing House.

Rapp, Donald. 2009. *Ice Ages and Interglacials Measurements, Interpretation, and Models.* Springer.

Redford, D. 2001. "Nut." *The Oxford Encyclopedia of Ancient Egypt*. USA: Oxford University Press.

Ridley, R. T. 2019. *Akhenaten: A Historian's View. The History of Ancient Egypt*. Cairo–New York: American University in Cairo Press.

Ritchie, Hannah, Pablo Rosado, and Max Roser. 2017. "Meat and Dairy Production." Our World in Data website (revised November 2019). In particular, see the graph titled "Yearly number of animals slaughtered for meat, World, 1961 to 2020."

Rosenstein, Nathan, and Robert Morstein-Marx. 2006. *A Companion to the Roman Republic*. Wiley.

Roth, Martha. 1997. *Law Collections from Mesopotamia and Asia Minor*. Atlanta: Society of Biblical Literature.

Roy, Christian. 2005. *Traditional Festivals: A Multicultural Encyclopedia*. Santa Barbara, Calif.: ABC-CLIO.

Rüpke, Jörg. 2007. *A Companion to Roman Religion: Sacrifices for Gods and Ancestors*. Blackwell.

Rushdoony, R. J. 1973. *The Institutes of Biblical Law*, vol. 1. Vallecito, Calif.: Chalcedon.

Sahagún, Bernardino De. 1577. *General History of the Things of New Spain. The Florentine Codex*.

Santo, Diana Espírito, et al. 2013. "Human Substances and Ontological Transformations in the African-Inspired Ritual Complex of Palo Monte in Cuba." *Critical African Studies*.

Savil, Diana. 2015. *Awakening the Flame: Igniting Your Potential Through the Power of the Violet Flame Chakra*. Bloomington, Ind.: Balboa Press.

Scerri, E. M., et al. 2018. "Did Our Species Evolve in Subdivided Populations across Africa, and Why Does It Matter?" *Cell* 33, no. 8: 582–94.

Schultz W. 2015. "Neuronal Reward and Decision Signals: From Theories to Data." *Physiological Reviews* 95, no. 3: 853–951.

Schürer, E. 1896. *A History of the Jewish People in the Time of Jesus Christ*, vol. 1. See "Herod the Great." New York: Scribner's.

ScienceDaily. 2011. "First Dogs Came from East Asia, Genetic Study Confirms." ScienceDaily website (November 28).

Sender, R., S. Fuchs, and R. Milo. 2016. "Revised Estimates for the Number of Human and Bacteria Cells in the Body." *PLOS Biology* 14, no. 8.

Sharma, C. 1962. *Indian Philosophy: A Critical Survey*. New York: Barnes & Noble.

Shastri, J. L., translator. 1950. *Siva Purana*. Part 1. New Delhi: Motilal Banarsidass.

Sheldrake, R. 2011. *The Presence of the Past: Morphic Resonance and the Habits of Nature*. London: Icon Books.

Shephard, S. 2012. *The Prophetic Seventy Weeks Solved*. Vancouver: Castle Publishing.

Shifman, Mikhail. 2012. *Advanced Topics in Quantum Field Theory*. Cambridge University Press.

Silver, C. B. 1998. *Strange and Secret Peoples: Fairies and Victorian Consciousness*. New York: Oxford University Press USA.

Singer, J. 1968. *Culture and the Collective Unconscious*. Evanston, Ill.: Northwestern University Press.

Slipher, V. M. 1913. "The Radial Velocity of the Andromeda Nebula." *Lowell Observatory Bulletin* 2, no. 8 (January 1): 56–57.

Spier, Fred. 2010. *Big History and the Future of Humanity*. Chichester: Wiley.

Stager, L., and S. R. Wolff. 1984. "Child Sacrifice at Carthage. Religious Rite or Population Control?" *Biblical Archaeology Review* 10:1.

Stahuljak, Z. 2013. *Pornographic Archaeology: Medicine, Medievalism, and the Invention of the French Nation*. Philadelphia: De Gruyter/University of Pennsylvania Press.

Steiner, Rudolf. *Nine Lectures on Bees*. 1923.

Sui, Choa Kok. 1992. *Advanced Pranic Healing*. Manila, Philippines: Institute for Inner Studies.

T & A Consulting. 2017. "Meat and Poultry Sector in India." Prepared for the Ministry of Foreign Relations of the Government of Brazil.

Taylor, M. 2016. "British Proslavery Arguments and the Bible, 1823–1833." *Slavery & Abolition* 37, no. 1: 139–58.

Thommen, Lukas. 2012. *An Environmental History of Ancient Greece and Rome*. Cambridge: Cambridge University Press.

Tomorad, M. 2015. "The Prohibition of Paganism in Egypt From the Middle of the 4th to the Middle of the 6th Century CE. The End of Ancient Egyptian Religion." *Journal of Egyptological Studies* 4:147–67.

Tudge, C. 1998. *Neanderthals, Bandits and Farmers: How Agriculture Really Began*. New Haven: Yale University Press.

Walcott, C. 1996. "Pigeon Homing: Observations, Experiments and Confusions." *Journal of Experimental Biology* 199 (Pt 1): 21–27.

Waldbaum, J. 1978. *From Bronze to Iron: The Transition From the Bronze Age to the Iron Age in the Eastern Mediterranean. Studies in Mediterranean Archaeology.* Philadelphia: Coronet Books.

Walker, M., et al. 2009. "Formal Definition and Dating of the Global Stratotype Section and Point For the Base of the Holocene Using the Greenland NGRIP Ice Core and Selected Auxiliary Records." *Journal of Quaternary Science* 24, no. 1: 3–17.

Wang, Yi'e. 2004. *Daoism in China.* China Intercontinental Press.

Watson, James L. 2011. *Ritual and Religion in Modern China: An Introduction.* New York: Bloomsbury Academic.

Wayne, R., and B. von Holdt. 2012. "Evolutionary Genomics of Dog Domestication." *Mammalian Genome* 23, no. 1–2: 3–18.

Wen, Xiao-Gan. 2004. *Quantum Field Theory of Many-Body Systems.* Oxford: Oxford University Press.

Werness, Hope B. 2006. *The Continuum Encyclopedia of Animal Symbolism in Art.* New York: Continuum.

White, D. 2012. *Freedom on My Mind: A History of African Americans with Documents.* Beech Cottage: Bedford Books.

Wilby, E. 2005. *Cunning Folk and Familiar Spirits: Shamanistic Visionary Traditions in Early Modern British Witchcraft and Magic.* Brighton: Sussex Academic Press.

Wilkinson, H. 1999. *Early Dynastic Egypt.* London: Routledge.

Wilkinson, John. 2016. *The Solar System in Close-Up.* Springer.

Willis, D. 1995. *Malevolent Nurture.* Ithaca, N.Y.: Cornell University Press.

Wilson, Horace, trans. 1866. *Rig Veda: A Collection of Ancient Hindu Hymns.* London: N. Trübner and Co. Available online.

Wiltschko, F. R., and W. Wiltschko. 2012. "Magnetoreception." In *Sensing in Nature. Advances in Experimental Medicine and Biology,* edited by C. Larrea. n. 739. Springer.

Wolchover, Natalie. 2012. "What If Humans Had Eagle Vision?" LiveScience website (February 24).

Woolfolk, Joanna Martine. 2012. *The Only Astrology Book You'll Ever Need.* Lanham, Md.: Rowman & Littlefield.

Xavier, Francisco Cândido. 1945 *Missionaries of the Light.* Brasilia: FEB.

———. 1939a. *On the Way to the Light.* Rio de Janeiro: FEB. Translated in 2011 by Darrel W. Kimble, Ily Reis, and Marcia Monica Saiz.

Xavier, Francisco Cândido, and Emmanuel. 1939b. "The Adamic Races." In *On the Way to the Light.* Brasilia: International Spiritist Council.

Yang, Carmen Emily. "What Is the Piezoelectric Effect?" Electronic Design website (Updated October 26, 2022).

Yuan, J., and R. Flad. 2005. "New Zoo-archaeological Evidence for Changes in Shang Dynasty Animal Sacrifice." *Journal of Anthropological Archaeology* 24, no. 3: 252–70.

Zeder, M. 2011. "The Origins of Agriculture in the Near East." *Current Anthropology* 52, no. S4: 221–35.

Zhao Y., and Q. Zhan. 2012a. "Electric Fields Generated by Synchronized Oscillations of Microtubules, Centrosomes and Chromosomes Regulate the Dynamics of Mitosis and Meiosis." *Theoretical Biology and Medical Modelling* 9, no. 26.

———. "Electric Oscillation and Coupling of Chromatin Regulate Chromosome Packaging and Transcription in Eukaryotic Cells." *Theoretical Biology and Medical Modelling* 9, no. 27.

# Index